AMERICAN BREAKDOWN

AMERICAN BREAKDOWN

The Trump Years and How They Befell Us

David Bromwich

VERSO

London • New York

First published by Verso 2019
© David Bromwich 2019

Earlier versions of the chapters originally appeared in the following publications, to which author and publisher would like to express their gratitude: Chapter 1, *New York Review of Books*, November 20, 2008; Chapter 2, *Harper's Magazine*, June 2015; Chapter 3, *London Review of Books*, February 16, 2017; Chapter 4, *London Review of Books*, July 13, 2017; Chapter 5, *London Review of Books*, August 9, 2018; Chapter 6, *London Review of Books*, March 7, 2019; Appendix A, *New York Review of Books*, November 10, 2016; Appendix B, *New York Review of Books*, April 10, 2017; Appendix C, *Guardian*, May 18, 2017

1 3 5 7 9 10 8 6 4 2

Verso
UK: 6 Meard Street, London W1F 0EG
US: 20 Jay Street, Suite 1010, Brooklyn, NY 11201
versobooks.com

Verso is the imprint of New Left Books

ISBN-13: 978-1-78873-726-5
ISBN-13: 978-1-78873-728-9 (US EBK)
ISBN-13: 978-1-78873-727-2 (UK EBK)

British Library Cataloguing in Publication Data
A catalogue record for this book is available from the British Library

Library of Congress Cataloging-in-Publication Data

Names: Bromwich, David, 1951– author.
Title: American breakdown : the Trump years and how they befell us / David Bromwich.
Description: London ; Brooklyn, NY : Verso, [2019] | Includes index.
Identifiers: LCCN 2019006674| ISBN 9781788737265 (hardback : alk. paper) | ISBN 9781788737272 (UK ebk.) | ISBN 9781788737289 (US ebk.)
Subjects: LCSH: Trump, Donald, 1946– | United States—Politics and government—21st century. | Political culture—United States—History—21st century.
Classification: LCC E912 .B76 2019 | DDC 973.933092—dc23
LC record available at https://lccn.loc.gov/2019006674

Typeset in the UK by Biblichor Ltd, Edinburgh
Printed and bound by CPI Group (UK) Ltd, Croydon, CR0 4YY

To Winifred Amaturo

When there was democracy, it was necessary to understand the character of the masses and how to control them. When the senate was in power, those who best knew its mind—the mind of the oligarchs—were considered the wisest experts on contemporary events. Similarly, now that Rome has virtually been transformed into an autocracy, the investigation and record of these details concerning the autocrat may prove useful. Indeed, it is from such studies—from the experience of others—that most men learn to distinguish right and wrong, advantage and disadvantage. Few can tell them apart instinctively.

— Tacitus, *Annals of Imperial Rome*

Contents

Introduction

This book is sent to press as the United States embarks on the third year of the Trump presidency; and, in the nature of the man and his government, a summary view is liable to mislead; for we are living with government by fiat, government by frenzy. The pace is relentless, there are no shock absorbers, and it takes luck as well as ingenuity to pick out the details that matter. What one can offer therefore is a series of contemporaneous snapshots, for the value they may carry as "present history." The chapters on Trump have the character of a political diary; they are dated accordingly and owe their interest to the record they keep of impressions marked by their moment. The chapters on Trump's immediate predecessors make a slightly weightier retrospective claim. The consideration of Cheney and Bush was written just three months before the end of their second term, and Obama was a lame-duck president facing a united

Republican Congress when I looked back in the spring of his seventh year. But Donald Trump is regarded by many people as a distinct phenomenon, an aberration that raises an urgent and unprecedented challenge. How did it happen?

You can take the story back to the mid-1930s, when the breakdown of constitutional democracy had already occurred in Italy and Germany and it was a fair question whether American democracy would survive the depression. But the political conditions of our crisis were put in place fifty-five years ago, with the expansion of the Vietnam War on a manufactured pretext: a spectral attack on two US ships and the Senate approval of the Gulf of Tonkin Resolution. The exposure of that deception, in the Pentagon Papers and elsewhere, prompted Americans in large numbers to suspect that their government couldn't be trusted. At the same time, elected representatives continued to cede enormous and ever-augmenting power to the presidency. In this subversion of constitutional balance, congressional majorities (wielded by both parties at different times) were guilty of constant and active complicity. Richard Nixon persisted in and secretly expanded the policy of Lyndon Johnson: bombing, defoliating, killing Vietnamese and requiring Americans to be killed. He defended the war with a mendacity and prosecuted it with a brutality as great as Johnson's, and with the same ultimate impotence. By the time of the US withdrawal in 1973— which coincided with the Watergate revelations and was soon followed by the exposure by a Senate committee of the long history of abuse of power at the CIA—the government itself was an object of thoroughgoing distrust. The presidency was as strong as ever.

To meet the oil crisis of the 1970s, President Carter promulgated a doctrine of US national interest in the Persian Gulf. It began to seem that the political business of the United States was congruent with the presidency, and the proper extent of American sovereignty coincided with the reach of American power. Ronald Reagan won the election of 1980 by portraying Carter as a weak leader, especially weak in his lack of concern with "preparedness," a charge substantiated by Carter's willingness to give the Panama Canal to Panama. This was the same strategy that John Kennedy had used against Nixon in 1960, with his talk of the "missile gap," and that George W. Bush would deploy against John Kerry in 2004. Discussion of foreign affairs since 1945—a period when the United States never *declared* a war—has been almost exclusively centered on war and the preparations for war. Always at the heart of such discussions is the political stance of the president.

No one did as much as Reagan to bend the popular language in which Americans think about government. Because of Reagan's simple faith and his genius as a salesman, that language, for a long generation now, has been centrally concerned with the rejection of government; with what every American should want to do and be able to do without any help from the government. It was as if, after the Vietnam War and in denial of the discouragement it brought, the American Dream gave birth to Reagan. Reagan, in turn, gave a delusionary afterlife to the dream. As an avuncular and beloved folk politician, he could seem a successor to Franklin Roosevelt; but it was a hollow imitation, cobbled together with the barest pretense of political understanding. An agreeable social type who felt no obligation to master the details of his own policies, Reagan opened up the possibility of the president-as-front-man. His successors in that job description have been George W. Bush and, in certain respects, Donald Trump: in the case of Bush, the engine in the rear was Vice President Cheney; in the case of Trump, the front itself is so erratically changeable that no driver seems able to master it for long. Reagan's casual contempt for government was of course an offense to the spirit of the Constitution; but as the promoter of a money-friendly attitude, he was a champion without parallel in American politics. He liked to say—it was a crowd-pleasing line for conservatives—"The nine most terrifying words in the English language are 'I'm from the government, and I'm here to help.'" That put the fantasy in a nutshell: if and when you realized the dream in your own life, it must have happened by your efforts alone. People could adopt the attitude without a second thought about the various good and useful jobs any modern government is relied on to carry out: food inspection, weather warnings, disaster relief, inter-state highways, airport security, the postal system, public schools, emergency medical aid. Reagan's order to remove the solar panels installed by President Carter on the roof of the White House—because they were a cosmetic nuisance—can stand for the irresponsibility with which his presidency launched the United States in a direction we have followed ever since. "Winning the Cold War"—an event (if it was an event) that many people believe Ronald Reagan brought about alone—gave his posthumous fame an enchantment peculiarly difficult to challenge.

George H. W. Bush was the bridge across which the United States walked to achieve domination of a unipolar world.

"Hegemony" became the favored euphemism for US commercial and ideological imposition, backed by the force of arms. The elder Bush's invasion of Panama in January 1990 served as a trial run for the first Gulf War in 1990 and 1991. Taken together, these ventures could be treated by the intelligence and military authorities as stress tests; and they were highly successful. The two-term presidency of Bill Clinton, so peaceful on its face, proceeded on a related path of domination by largely commercial means, with methods that combined ideological and economic pressure. Under Clinton, the eastward expansion of NATO—in violation of a promise made by George H. W. Bush to Mikhail Gorbachev—added a species of veiled military pressure to the capitalist "shock therapy" prescribed by American economists for the radical reform of Russia and countries of the former Eastern Bloc. This planting of trans-European trip wires for a possible conflict—the renewed Cold War alliance in the absence of the Cold War threat—was a reflexive act by the policy and military elite of the United States, the UK, and Europe. Only in retrospect can we see it as the sleep-walking provocation it represented to a Russian nationalist like Vladimir Putin. The message was simple. The United States and its obedient allies would continue to oppose Russia as if it were the Soviet Union, unless a client politician on the pattern of Boris Yeltsin could be found to cooperate without protest and be grateful for the shock therapy. The contents of the policy were mass privatization and fast-track market capitalism. The generous guidance that the United States provided to Russia (such was the rough draft of hegemony) would eventually be extended to every other country in the world, no matter how adequate its previous arrangements, no matter how resistant its customs and culture to the ways of Wall Street and the World Bank.

Bush Sr. had nonetheless incurred resentment in Republican foreign policy circles for his comparative restraint in dealing with Russia, as well as his firmness in warning Israel against an expansionist settlement policy. Bill Clinton proved more amenable to the consensus and, while still a candidate, gave his assurance to the Israel lobby that he was answerable to their concerns. He signed the Antiterrorism and Effective Death Penalty Act of 1996, in the wake of the Oklahoma City bombing, which radically curbed habeas corpus protections. This was a strong precursor of the Patriot Act of 2001, which Congress would pass the month after the terrorist attack on the World Trade Center and the national panic that ensued. The year 1996 also saw Clinton's approval of legislation "to end welfare as we know it"—a tribute to the continuing hold of the Reagan anti-government attitude. Shock therapy had come home.

In domestic politics, Clinton was burdened with fighting the Contract with America, a feverish anti-constitutional cause spearheaded in the 1994 midterm elections by the veteran Georgia representative Newt Gingrich. The terms of the Contract assumed (in defiance of federalist doctrine that the Republican Party from the mid-nineteenth to the mid-twentieth century had seemed to inherit) the sanctity and absolute authority of popular mandates over the local, timely, individual judgments of representatives in the House or Senate. By holding the signatories to the literal conditions of a preexisting formula, the Contract embodied a self-denying ordinance, akin to Robespierre's experiment in 1791, and it contained a similar provision requiring the signers not to seek re-election. The last condition proved the most chimerical of the pledges; and in his attempt to close down the government, Gingrich was outmaneuvered by Clinton. Still, he had shown that it could be a popular gesture to nullify the deliberative function of government itself.

These were "loomings," as Melville called them. The truly catastrophic event in American life after the Second World War has proved to be the invention by George W. Bush and his co-president, Dick Cheney, of the global war on terror—a war intended to last for generations. Its first episode was to be a successful invasion and short occupation of Iraq, on the pretext of removing weapons of mass destruction. From there, the design for a "clean break" with previous policy called for the overthrow, whether by military force or proxy insurgency, of the governments of Iran and Syria. Quite possibly, for visionaries like Cheney and his associates Paul Wolfowitz and Douglas Feith, the new-modeled Eastern advantages of NATO figured in the longer game: a strategy that might eventually produce regime change in Russia. The actual sequel is before us. Eighteen years after the US invasion of Afghanistan to hunt down and punish Osama bin Laden and install a secular government, and sixteen years after the United States bombed, invaded, and occupied Iraq, both decisions have led to unending calamity. We no longer call it the global war on terror. It is the forever war.

One sure sign of the bad faith of the war is that we can't bear to hear about it. Long ago, respectable newspapers took it off their front pages; they have felt free to let it vanish for weeks at a time; the same is true of the television, radio, and digital media outlets that attempt to be carriers of responsible news. In 2018, the United States bombed or assisted attacks in nine countries in the Greater Middle East: Afghanistan, Iraq, Pakistan, Yemen, Syria, Somalia, Niger, Sudan, and Mali. Nor was this a function chiefly of the recklessness of Donald Trump. For the most part, Trump has only done what the defense, intelligence, and state department professionals, the path-of-least-resistance advisers, told him to do. Barack Obama did the same before him.

I came of age during the Vietnam War, and my earliest political activity was in the anti-war movement in 1966. What the United States did to Vietnam goes beyond any subsequent catastrophes we have inflicted, even in Iraq. But it was the beginning of a pattern of intervention that never stopped for long in the thirty-nine years that separated Bush and Cheney's war of 2003 from LBJ's escalation in 1964. I began to write political commentaries with some regularity in 2002 when it seemed to me the country was in a fever, that it was "out of itself" (to borrow a phrase from Burke), and that we had pushed aside too quickly the democratic resources of collective deliberation and self-restraint. With the Iraq invasion in 2003, I believed (to borrow a phrase from Stephen Walt) my country had driven off a cliff. We are now plodding ahead, dispatching missiles as we go, several thousand feet below that cliff, as if the cratered roads that branch off in all directions were our usual terrain. Few Americans venture an upward glance and recognize that a life might still be possible at that earlier altitude. Our refusal to consult and learn from a different kind of map has prevented our finding a way back.

Barack Obama's path to the presidency involved a conscious determination to become the world's number-one celebrity. He succeeded: the fruits of his success appear in the titles of post-presidency books like the memoir *Thanks, Obama*, the photo-album *Hugs from Obama*, and the anthology of letters *To Obama: With Love, Joy, Anger, and Hope*. His care for the well-being of people was real enough, but, as a series of changes-of-stance in 2009 demonstrated, his intention to pull back from the war on terror could never bear much strain. He gave Americans an era of remission after the continuous shock of the Bush-Cheney government, and the comfort of his presence answered with emollient ease the question: What has befallen us? By his poise and self-possession, his air of unconcern at attacks by political enemies, his love of leisure and of serious talk, Obama allowed us to pretend that none of it ever happened. In his power to nurture a fantasy congenial to American self-love, he was the successor of Reagan (whom he admired for having understood that symbolism can matter more than actions). But in wielding the power of celebrity to magnetize attention, Obama was also the precursor of Trump: a fact initially hard to digest because of the polar opposition of their characters and the different media they stood at the center of. For Obama, the venue of choice was the solemn speech, the talk-show appearance, the flattering full-length interview by a tame reporter. For Trump, it is his daily tweets and the occasional boisterous address to a packed stadium. Again, Obama's personality answered to the common idea of what it means to be judicious, temperate, and agreeable. The selfish motive that is so conspicuous in Trump, and the frequent brutality of his language, make an utterly contrary appeal.

The plan for the war on terror had been a product of the mind of Cheney working on the susceptibility of the younger Bush. On the one hand, the craving for secrecy, order, and acts of executive power that brooked no opposition; on the other hand, the need for simplicity, the love of battle from a distance, intoxicating emotions, and an evangelical cause as irrefutable as a home team to cheer for. Obama gave up the name "war on terror"—he preferred to speak vaguely of "this war we're in"—but never took the major step of renouncing the project itself. The tools for a worldwide constabulary mission had been fashioned and reserved for the chief executive under Cheney and Bush. With Obama, the methods of violence were reformed in public and extended behind the scenes; and on points of constitutional principle, he betrayed, early on, a readiness to retreat. When, in May 2009, he announced the resettlement in northern Virginia of seventeen Uighur Muslims who had been wrongly detained in Guantánamo, the angry reaction of Frank Wolf, the Republican representative of the tenth congressional district, was all it took to abort the plan. When, six months later, Obama's attorney general announced that the Islamist Khalid Sheikh Mohammed would be tried in a federal court in New York City for conspiracy to commit the September 11 attack, objections by Mayor Bloomberg, and by interested partisans of the war on terror, were allowed to simmer and come to a boil; and having vowed to replace military tribunals with constitutional justice, Obama called off the intended reform. A thoroughgoing practice of euphemism was in fact his largest innovation in the conduct of the war. Thus the murder of bin Laden by US special forces was turned into the sentence:

"We delivered justice to bin Laden." As the neoconservative editor and publicist William Kristol pointed out, by 2011 Obama had made it clear he was executing "the policies people like me had been advocating for quite a while"; the Fox News commentator Greg Gutfeld added the relevant list: "We've got the drones. We've got military tribunals. We've got Gitmo. We're bombing Libya. People who voted for Obama got four more years of Bush."

Obama's National Archives speech of May 2009 and the decision, that November, to send 30,000 additional troops to Afghanistan, signaled the termination of his resolve to check the military adventurism and pull in the national security policies of the Bush-Cheney government. Instead, health care legislation would be his legacy. The welfare-state domestic emphasis—on the drawing board for the Democratic Party over the previous half-century—was strangely mismatched to a country in crisis alike from the post-2001 terrorism panic and the financial collapse of 2008; but the choice was well suited to Obama's temperament. He radiated good and gentle intentions, along with an unspecified hope, which he could symbolize equally to Americans and to the world. Throughout his presidency he seemed happiest when addressing and embracing fellow citizens in need; he would be the one to offer them solace (a favorite word); and he could do it in all of the many non-presidential roles he inhabited: teacher, pastor, moderator of a "conversation" about one thing or another, and (perhaps most important) grief counselor.

He had always been at heart a motivational speaker: he delivered orations after the mass murders at Fort Hood, Aurora, Tucson, Newtown, Boston, and Charleston; and he was photographed personally consoling sufferers from Hurricane Sandy, Hurricane Irene, and other catastrophes of the global climate disruption—a subject about which he made no general statement in the middle years of his presidency, because he considered it a political loser. Unlike Trump, he did acknowledge the reality of the danger; he would finally help to push through and sign the Paris climate accord; but the diplomatic achievement was accompanied by no effort to educate American opinion. The same pattern of international agreement in the absence of national persuasion could be discerned in Obama's conduct of the Iran nuclear deal. He defended it well, in the most closely argued and courageous speech of his presidency; but even there, a treaty was presented in rhetorical terms that presumed everlasting hostility. By blocking a determined enemy from the production of a nuclear weapon, he argued, the United States was doing the most we could to protect Americans. Even after the Iranian people had elected as their president the non-fanatical Hassan Rouhani, the nuclear deal put off to an unthinkable future the very idea of improved relations with Iran.

The end of the Iraq war was announced by Obama in October 2011; he would declare three years later, in an interview with the *New Yorker*, that al-Qaeda was so reduced it was now obliged to field its "JV team." Unfortunately, he made this claim (with a jaunty athleticism recalling the younger Bush) at a time when ISIS had already raised its flag over Mosul and Raqqa. He likewise called an official close to the US commitment in Afghanistan, before dispatching a new round of troops when military advisers told him to. Again, in 2011 he emulated Bush's performance in Iraq by supplying the Libyan rebels with continuous air support—a disastrous misjudgment that, in a matter of months, would lead to civil war and the mass migration of refugees across the Mediterranean Sea. Though Obama cultivated the good opinion of neoconservatives like Kristol and Robert Kagan, he did such things not mainly to propitiate them, but rather in conformity with the strategic thinking of neoliberals like his secretary of state Hillary Clinton, his national security adviser Susan Rice, his UN ambassador Samantha Power, and the strategist Anne-Marie Slaughter. If one gave much credit to his show of verbal restraint, this presentation could seem the opposite of the adventurism of Bush and Cheney; the reverse, too, of Donald Trump tweeting provocations at the top of his voice and pretending to want wars (with North Korea, with China) he had no desire to fight. Obama, on the contrary, kept up a consistent façade of reluctance to fight the very wars he was protracting. A fair portion of the energy of the Obama White House was given to keeping those wars off the front page. Whole weeks went by when a reader of the *New York Times* or the *Washington Post* or a watcher of MSNBC or CNN would hardly imagine the United States was still engaged in bombing and drone-fired missile strikes, conventional firefights and black-ops assassinations. Nor that Obama's Middle East legacy to Trump was going to include extensive military, logistical, and intelligence support for the Saudi destruction of Yemen.

Hillary Clinton in 2016 ran largely on the strength of Obama's achievement in health care and the non-divisive tone he set for the country. She adopted his pledge of concern for ordinary people, "the middle class" (Democrats by now had struck from their lexicon the words "poor" and "poverty"). She found numberless ways of reminding voters that she was not Trump. But Hillary Clinton was a politician oddly deficient in political talent. About none of her array of talking points and positions could a half-informed voter nod and feel, "Yes, she understands the problems I'm having." Whereas the brash sloganeering of Trump against immigration, in favor of "bringing back jobs" and cutting off the US military commitments and trade alliances that people held responsible for the loss of lives and jobs—all these would prompt immediate recognition in the many contested states of that election.

Trump acts from motives that are intelligible at a glance. He cares for money and publicity, each for the sake of the other. Loyalty matters to him more than laws. For loyalty can be counted on to protect corruption, and without corruption there will be less money. In Trump's first two years in office, the United States became more entangled in the Middle East than it had been under Obama; the fighting continued in Afghanistan, in Iraq, in Syria, in Libya; ties were strengthened with Saudi Arabia and Israel, but this could only mean new trip wires for another war in the region. American respect for alliances that had held steady since 1945 he shrugged off with an unseemly scorn; Trump appeared to think such organizations a useless remnant of the Cold War: they could safely be allowed to atrophy. And yet, in many ways he was a domestic president, too, and the largest political result of his election was the passage of the tax bill that drove up his approval ratings in the early months of 2018—a time when that encouragement was

badly needed. It was a bill that any other Republican president, attuned to the morale of the party in 2017, would
have had to support; and in the nature of its scheduled
changes, in a few years it will benefit only the rich. The
other accomplishment Trump is fond of citing, a significant
decrease in the numbers of the unemployed, is not for the
most part his doing; his promise of a large-scale return of
American manufacturing is still unrealized; and his baffling
appointment of the militarists John Bolton and Mike
Pompeo as national security adviser and secretary of state
calls into question the meaning of his resolution to stay out
of unnecessary wars.

All along, his pledge to withdraw from our wars in the
Greater Middle East had been accompanied by a demagogic
readiness for conflict of other sorts: a trade war with China,
for example, and regime change in Iran (the latter no different from what Bush and Cheney hoped to realize in 2007,
and what Benjamin Netanyahu wanted Obama to support
in 2010–2011). But if the essence of Trump is chaos, his
spasmodic exertions of command and control have never
slackened since he announced his candidacy in 2015. His
tweets (an average of five per day) of course receive mixed
responses, but they keep him at center stage from day to
day and almost from hour to hour. From his commercial
perspective, all business is good business: at no moment is
Trump not a leading topic of news or public commentary;
the mainstream media have profited financially by this diet
of all-day Trump; the networks and papers know it, and the
public does, too. It is something like the hold of the repulsive charlatan over the captive crowd in Thomas Mann's
Italian allegory of the thirties, *Mario and the Magician*, or

the curse that binds a dinner party chattering interminably against their will in a single room in Luis Buñuel's grotesque comedy *The Exterminating Angel*. Trump has commandeered the mainstream media by his occupation of social media; in doing so, he has changed, from the bottom up, the way Americans think about politics—something none of his more coherent predecessors had managed. Politics has become a series of fast reactions, and the anti-Trump swarm that dominates the mainstream media are at once his victims, his beneficiaries, and his accomplices.

I confess to having been initially skeptical, not of a Trump connection to Russia, but of any clear and traceable pipeline from the Trump campaign back to the Russian government. This largely speculative theory became an obsession of liberal commentators and journalists as soon as Trump took office—pushed by the defeated Hillary Clinton, by the TV news host Rachel Maddow, and by well-placed Democratic lawmakers like Adam Schiff and Mark Warner. They believed that Russia could well have swung the election for Trump; and fairly often they seemed to attach a corollary: it was a moral imperative for the United States, in retaliation, to pass severer sanctions, send more arms to NATO, and subvert the Russian interest in Syria even if that meant prolonging the war. Most of the people who talked on these lines were too young to have experienced the madness of the Cold War. (If you were under fifty-four on the day Trump was elected, you hadn't been born at the time of the Cuban Missile Crisis.) Yet, from the sheer weight and mass of the circumstantial evidence, it must now be acknowledged that collaboration between the

Trump campaign and Russian business, intelligence, and political actors seems extremely likely.

Trump is surrounded by such evidence—entangled in coils that no effort of the most strenuous legal ingenuity could possibly relieve him of. By November 30, 2018, his first national security adviser, Michael Flynn, had pleaded guilty to lying to the FBI (having also lied about his Russia negotiations to several persons in the White House, including the vice president). Three months earlier, Paul Manafort, Trump's second campaign manager, had been found guilty in a federal court in Virginia on charges of tax and bank fraud stemming from his work for Ukrainian politicians; it later emerged that Manafort too had lied to the FBI about his use of a Russian liaison, Konstantin Kilimnik, to convey election polling data to two Russian oligarchs. Meanwhile, Donald Trump Jr. has been in the public eye as a plausible target of prosecution for his Trump Tower meeting with Russians who offered to share damaging information on Hillary Clinton. In December, Trump's lawyer Michael Cohen pleaded guilty of having lied to Congress about plans for Trump Tower Moscow, which, contrary to his testimony, did overlap with the period of the campaign. The fact that existing sanctions against Russia would have interfered with that cherished Trump project may explain Flynn's pre-inaugural contact with Russian authorities about an early lifting of sanctions in the new administration. Still another member of the Trump campaign network, George Papadopoulos, pleaded guilty to making false statements to the FBI about his connection with Russian agents during the campaign itself. Roger Stone and Jerome Corsi— the former an adept of dirty tricks going back to the Nixon years, the latter a "birther" propagandist against Obama—have signified their loyalty to Trump, and Trump has reminded them of his power to pardon, but they are vulnerable for their apparent advance information on the release of hacked materials from the Democratic National Committee. By January 25, Stone had been indicted and arrested.

This is only a partial list. What carries conviction is the pattern of interested cooperation. In all the extended train of characters and meetings, careful and careless hints and confidences, which make up the myriad relationships between the Trump campaign and Russians of one description or another (lawyers, diplomats, media impresarios, oligarchs, agents), not a single knock on a door by Russia was greeted with anything but an eager "Come in." It is inconceivable that none of these contacts was cleared with the man at the head of the campaign—the candidate, Donald Trump—and inconceivable that a refusal by Trump would have been overridden by persons lower down the ladder to pursue the risky business on their own. The largest single category of evidence, however, remains the sacking by Trump of federal prosecutors he knew to be involved in investigations that might lead to his being charged with a crime. On transparently ad-lib pretexts or for contradictory reasons or for no admitted cause, Trump fired the deputy attorney general Sally Yates (January 30, 2017); the US attorney for the southern district of New York, Preet Bharara (March 11, 2017); the director of the FBI, James Comey (May 9, 2017); and his own attorney general, Jeff Sessions (November 7, 2018). All circumstances taken together, it adds up to a practice of obstruction of justice as consistent and penetrable as the actions that triggered the charge of obstruction in the articles of impeachment drawn up against Richard Nixon.

One may recognize Trump's complicity with Russian financial and state interests without pretending to be shocked by each new revelation, or accepting a re-militarized policy as an appropriate response to the Russian attempt to influence American voters. Such intrusions in the form of surveillance, subsidy, or infiltration are hardly foreign to the habits of the US government—targeting elections in Russia, Georgia, or Ukraine, for example—and Americans have been on the wrong end of it before. (Consider the less successful but far bolder machinations of the Israel lobby in arranging Netanyahu's speech to Congress and Romney's trip to Jerusalem to influence the 2012 election.) Trump has driven some of his most resolute opponents to think it is policy enough to place a minus sign beside whatever he does. Might it be desirable for the United States to reach a long-term understanding with North Korea? To withdraw troops from Syria once ISIS is defeated? To renew a limited collaboration with Russia in order to avoid nuclear war and control the proliferation of nuclear materials and technology? Even in matters of such importance, Russian-American cooperation had lapsed in 2014 under pressure of the US reaction to hostilities in Ukraine and the Russian annexation of Crimea—actions the United States was bound to condemn but which were predictable, so long as one grants that there is such a thing as a Russian sphere of influence. In the eyes of most of the world, everything the United States has done in the Middle East since 2001 and much of what it did in Central America in the 1980s is a great deal harder to defend.

The war party of 2003–2006 has resurrected itself in the United States, as a kind of shadow state department, and is now propounding a version of imperial internationalism to counter the isolationism of Trump. The tendency has two wings, one neoconservative, the other neoliberal, both promoting a return to US leadership by force of democracy and arms. The neoconservative advocacy group, called the Alliance for Securing Democracy, has on its board Michael Chertoff, Mike Rogers, and Bill Kristol; the neoliberal version, National Security Action, includes the Obama speechwriter Ben Rhodes, the Obama national security adviser Tom Donilon, Susan Rice, and Anne-Marie Slaughter; while Jake Sullivan, who was in line to be Hillary Clinton's national security advisor, is on the advisory council of the first group and serves as co-chair of the second. What all these people desiderate is a larger and more constant US presence in the world. The neoconservatives may look for armies and special ops and regimes to change; the neoliberals may prefer trade deals; but there will be plenty of conferences where academics, think-tank pundits, and generals can safely mingle. "We have," as William Arkin observed, "a single war party in the United States and it's the only party that's given voice."

Where does this leave us? There is an outlaw presidency, the first in American history to say so almost on its face. Every day brings fresh evidence of an administration conceived and executed as a money-making scheme; and it betrays its character when it reverts to the argot of the gangster world—the world that created Trump through his contacts in the New York real estate milieu. One of Roy

Cohn's associates memorably said, "I double-cross myself twice a day just to keep in practice." Trump's habit of saying X and Not X, close together, displays obedience to this precept by a financial athlete who must never break training. When the Saudi murder of the journalist Jamal Khashoggi could no longer be doubted, Trump said: "They had a very bad original concept, it was carried out poorly, and the cover-up was one of the worst cover-ups in the history of cover-ups"—the verdict of a contest judge demoting a failed performance in a delicate genre. Trump assimilates all politics to the dispatching of flunkies and payoffs to protect corruption. Two recent books on the first year of his presidency—Bob Woodward's *Fear* and Michael Wolff's *Fire and Fury*—are replete with examples.

To dwell on the criminal habits, however, is to leave out of account the debased form of celebrity to which Trump has accustomed his political audience, and by which he retains his hold on the media and the nation. He is a president who gets on all fours with citizens, to praise flatterers and accomplices, to denounce or deprecate enemies, and to wheedle with persons who stand somewhere between. From his position as chief magistrate, he addresses promises and threats *to individual citizens*. All this he does in public, and does with an incurable shamelessness. A personality of his temper as president could not have seemed a distant possibility to the constitutional framers. Trump differs in kind from even the most undistinguished of his predecessors, since his overt message is that we can choose to be ignorant—ignorant of science, ignorant of the law, ignorant of the logic of non-contradiction. When President Reagan said that the most dreaded words in the language came from the government official who wanted to help, he was pandering, no doubt, but it was a joke well suited to an ideology in which he actually believed. The same cannot be said of Trump. He has no interest in government, large or small, and no commitment to ideals of any description.

The Constitution seems the best native resource for a political recovery, and the hardest to traduce. Its prohibition of external emoluments given to an official of the government; the explanation of causes that could justify impeachment, and the procedures to be followed; above all (abandoned but not gone) the explicit framing of the role of the Senate in approving and, where necessary, overruling a president's decisions in foreign policy—all these things bear looking into. But though impeachment is the constitutional solution, it may be that only a rejection of Trump by a strong majority in 2020 could begin to reverse the degeneration that he personified as a symptom even before he hastened the process by his official acts. The loyal Tea Party remnant have been so thoroughly imposed on that they would take impeachment as proof of a conspiracy against Trump. They have been coached to believe that every finding of the Mueller inquiry is part of an organized attempt to nullify the election of 2016.

Occasionally, in the chapters that follow, I bring up the fact that foreign policy limits what can be done in domestic policy. This is most the case for a nation immersed in multiple wars of choice. Whether we speak of them or not, they are a drain on civic imagination and public energy, to say nothing of the loss of lives. Nationalism, of the sort Trump seemed to represent in his campaign, might at least have led to a greater concentration on the repair and reform of

American society, and the improvement of justice at home. But as Michael Lewis showed in *The Fifth Risk*, the most dire hazard of the corporate plunder of the Trump administration can be seen in defunding and staff reductions in places like the National Weather Service (located in the Department of Commerce), food and drug regulation (the Department of Agriculture), and control of nuclear waste (the Department of Energy). The greatest war we face for many generations to come will be defensive in nature. Climate disruption stands as the overwhelming collective danger that the distraction of the Trump years has tempted us to ignore; and those who concentrate all their passions on Trump are captive to his denial as much as those who are genuinely ignorant. Global climate disruption is already a cause of effects we still speak of as if they belonged to separate categories—immigration, inequality, war. There will be wars as a consequence of climate disruption, there will be mass migrations, and there will be increased inequality. Meeting the change that is on us will require a form of international control we haven't begun to imagine. Trump did more than anyone else to create a national distemper that has postponed for a few years longer a reckoning with the future of life on earth. More than cheating in an election or insulting traditional allies or degrading the norms of public speech in unheard-of ways, his denial of the existence of this more-than-national predicament should be counted the largest of his crimes.

I

The Cheney Co-Presidency

November 2008

When George W. Bush testified before the 9/11 Commission, Dick Cheney was with him in the Oval Office. What was said there remains a secret, but throughout the double session, it appears, Cheney deferred to Bush. Aides to the president afterward explained that the two men had to sit together for people to see how fully Bush was in control. A likelier motive was the obvious one: they had long exercised joint command but neither knew exactly how much the other knew, or what the other would say in response to particular questions. Bush also brought Cheney for the reason that a witness under oath before a congressional committee may bring along his lawyer. He could not risk an answer that his adviser might prefer to correct. Yet Bush would scarcely have changed the public understanding of their relationship had he sent in Cheney alone. "When you're talking to Dick Cheney," the president said in 2003, "you're talking to me."

The shallowest charge against Cheney is that he somehow inserted himself into the vice presidency by heading the team that examined other candidates for the job. He used the position deviously, so the story goes, to sell himself to the credulous younger Bush. The truth is both simpler and more strange. Since 1999, Cheney had been one of a group of political tutors of Bush, including Condoleezza Rice and Paul Wolfowitz; in this company, Bush found Cheney especially congenial—not least his way of asserting his influence without ever stealing a scene. Bush, too, resembled Cheney in preferring to let others speak, but he lacked the mind and patience for discussions: virtues that Cheney possessed in abundance.

As early as March 2000, Bush asked him whether he would consider taking the second slot. Cheney at first said no. Later, he agreed to serve as Bush's inspector of the qualifications of others; his lieutenants were his daughter Liz and David Addington. Some way into that work, Bush asked Cheney again, and this time he said yes. The understanding was concluded before any of the lesser candidates were interviewed. It was perhaps the first public deception that they worked at together: a lie of omission—and a trespass against probity—to give an air of legitimacy to the search for a nominee. But their concurrence in the stratagem, and the way each saw the other hold to its terms, signaled an equality in manipulation as no formal contract could have done. It is hardly likely that an exchange of words was necessary.

The vice-presidential search in the spring of 2000 was characteristic of the co-presidency to come in one other way. It involved the collection of information for future use against political rivals. In this case, the rivals were the other potential VPs, among them Lamar Alexander, Chuck Hagel, and Frank Keating. They had been asked to submit exhaustive data concerning friends, enemies, sexual partners, psychological vicissitudes (noting all visits to therapists of any kind), personal embarrassments, and sources of possible slander, plus a complete medical history. Each also signed a notarized letter that gave Cheney the power to request records from doctors without further clearance.

All this information would prove useful in later years. Barton Gellman reveals in *Angler* that soon after Frank Keating was mentioned as a likely candidate for attorney general, a story appeared in *Newsweek* about an awkward secret in his past: an eccentric patron had paid for his children's college education. No law had been broken, and nothing wrongly concealed; but the story killed a chance for Keating to be named attorney general, and the leak could only have come from one person. Doubtless most of the secrets in Cheney's possession were the more effective for not being used.

Cheney by nature is a high functionary and inside operative, ready to learn and eager to ferret out the background of people and events, both the things he is supposed to know and the things he is not. It is symptomatic that in the Ford administration, when Cheney served as White House chief of staff, he declined a generous offer of cabinet status: higher visibility, he believed, would only diminish his actual potency. By the end of his time in that office, he had narrowed down access to the president to the people he himself preferred; and at his retirement, Cheney's staff gave him, as Stuart Spencer recalls, "a bicycle wheel with all the spokes busted out except for one—his."

A now forgotten aberration of the Republican convention in 1980 may have helped to crystalize his thinking about the advantages of a recessive stance. For a few frantic days that summer, it looked as if Ronald Reagan would need someone with demonstrable experience on the ticket if he was to have a chance in November; and there were serious discussions of a co-presidency to be shared between Reagan and Ford. Cheney, a close adviser to Ford, was an interested witness, and he saw how the excess and literalness of Ford's "wish list" for vice-presidential powers caused the negotiations to break down. Still, this was a tantalizingly close call; and it could only have left Cheney thoughtful about future possibilities. Suppose one day the Republican Party nominated another charmer, cut out, like Reagan, for the getting of votes but as fundamentally uninterested as Reagan was in the actual running of government.

No two persons and indeed no twenty in Reagan's administration enjoyed the power that Cheney settled into in 2001; but the role of the president in these two administrations has been much the same. He is the campaigner, the crowd-pleaser (if he can), the known presence at the visible desk who signs the laws and executive orders. The amiability of George W. Bush has turned out to be less versatile and translatable than Reagan's: the boyish vulgar humor and back-slapping require easy success as a precondition; and apart from the three and a half years after the September 11 attacks—the period of the "fast wars" and the "war presidency"—his two terms in office have been marked by conspicuous failures.

Bush's exceedingly low spirits have been palpable now for many months; and without the one to two hours of strenuous exercise that are the heart of his day, his mental state would surely be a good deal grimmer. And yet, for this very reason the growing evidence about Cheney's bad judgments has not greatly diminished Bush's reliance on him. If the vice president dominates policy less than he did before 2006, the reason is only that others around Bush have become more confident. It remains nonetheless a relationship without any parallel in American history. "The vice president," as Jacob Weisberg observes in *The Bush Tragedy*, "built his power over Bush by finding ways to give power to Bush." There has never been a moment in this administration when the dependency let up.

Something subtly changed in Dick Cheney between 1995 and 2000, some equilibrium or inward balance of ambition and ordinary prudence. These were his years as CEO of Halliburton, where he did not post enormous profits: his decision, in 1998, to merge Halliburton with Dresser Industries and the subsequent asbestos claims against Dresser led the value of Halliburton stock to fall from $54 to $9 a share between August and December 2000.

Yet Cheney as CEO had a value as great as that of any official who has passed through the revolving door that separates government office from corporate chairmanships. His importance was as a connection maker, a facilitator, a speculative explorer of large innovations. While at Halliburton, Cheney would commission a study of the utility of employing private security contractors to fight in wars—only a piece of "research" at the time, but it would pay later for both the company and the vice president, with the off-the-books contracts that by privatizing state protection kept much of the Iraq occupation out of public view.

These were the years, too, of Dick Cheney's close association with the American Enterprise Institute and its offspring, the Project for the New American Century. The parent think tank, once an ordinary home for postwar business conservatism, had mutated, under the guidance of Irving Kristol, into the most lavish and energetic of the quasi-academic lobbies of neoconservative doctrine. The AEI, in the late 1970s and the early 1980s, had been transformed into an institute for the promotion of laissez-faire economics, militarized foreign policy, and the dismantling of the welfare state. It differed from, say, the Rand Corporation in eschewing any claim to impartiality of analysis. It was polemical and took confrontational positions that were disseminated early in the lectures and seminars open to resident fellows. The AEI differed, also, from an older centrist policy outfit like the Brookings Institution in having superior access to the mass media, thanks to careful self-advertisement and the coaching that its representatives often received from editors and agents such as Adam Bellow and Lynn Chu. A more-in-sorrow style was favored in discussing the grim necessity, for example, of increasing America's nuclear stockpile or stopping the "culture of poverty" in the black community by cutting off federal programs.

Cheney's familiarity with the policy institute way of talking was a steady and not a negligible factor in his

ability to gain acceptance for his most outlandish maneu-
vers in the years between 2001 and 2003: the tax cuts and
no-bid contracts with the Pentagon; withdrawal of the
United States from the Anti-Ballistic Missile Treaty; the
sudden commitment of the Pentagon to vast expenditures
on missile defense, notwithstanding the record of test
failures among missiles engendered by the Star Wars
program under Reagan; the systematic exaggeration of
the menace of Saddam Hussein in order to build support
for a war against Iraq; and, in the triumphal mood of
April 2003, the refusal to consider diplomatic contacts
with Iran to obtain a "Grand Bargain" for peace in the
Middle East.

Yet to those who knew the language, Cheney was only
the forward edge of a policy long in the works. It had been
announced almost in public in the turn-of-the-century
strategy document *Rebuilding America's Defenses*, the most
substantial work commissioned by the Project for the New
American Century. Like the sponsors of that treatise—
among them Paul Wolfowitz, Lewis "Scooter" Libby,
William Kristol, Frederick Kagan, and Stephen Cambone—
and like the adepts of American hegemony at the AEI,
Cheney, before he took office as vice president, had
concluded that there were no necessary limits on US
domination of the world. This conviction hardened during
the Clinton years—a window of time, as neoconservatives
sometimes say, in which America could have asserted far
more control than it did, and with a freer military hand.
Cheney's institutional prowess, and his readiness to execute
policies long in the making, point to a larger pattern that
James Mann wrote well about in *Rise of the Vulcans*.

Republicans, since 1975, have had a foreign policy establishment that stays in place even when they are out of
power. (The Democrats can claim nothing of the sort.)
Through the continuity of neoconservative advisers, the
military-statist wing of the Republican Party has thus, for
three decades now, had the consistency and coherence of a
shadow government. Though remarked by no one at the
time, most of its essential policies—including "force projection" in the Middle East and continued pressure on Russia
in spite of the fall of communism—were already in place by
1996, when the leading foreign policy adviser to Bob Dole
was Paul Wolfowitz.

The Cheney doctrine of preventive war was first
announced in a document called *Defense Planning Guidance*, drafted in 1992 by Zalmay Khalilzad (now US
ambassador to the UN after serving as ambassador to Iraq)
and revised by Lewis Libby. This guide was cleared for
public release in early 1993 by Cheney in his final days as
George H. W. Bush's secretary of defense. Cheney took
considerable pride in the prescription here that the United
States should "act against" emerging threats "before they
are fully formed." George W. Bush would still be echoing
those phrases in his June 2002 commencement address at
West Point: "We must take the battle to the enemy, disrupt
his plans, and confront the worst threats before they
emerge." Richard Perle saying "we have no time to lose"
(July 11, 2002) and Cheney himself telling the Veterans of
Foreign Wars that "time is not on our side" (August 26,
2002) kept up the same drumbeat with the same theory to
support them. *Defense Planning Guidance* conferred on
America the right to launch at will an international war of

aggression. As for the larger strategy, extractable from *Rebuilding America's Defenses*, it was marked by an overriding ambition for global mastery, for the possession of irresistible military forces, for an expanded arsenal of nuclear weapons, and for large new investments in missile defense. These publications of 1993 and 2000 now seem a pair of symbolic brackets around the neoconservative exile that was the Clinton administration. All along, this was the normal thinking around the AEI and the Cheney circle. Yet when placed alongside the norms of the containment policy during the years 1946–1989, the new dogma betrayed a shift so tremendous that it could not have been ratified without a layer of well-instructed opinion makers to prepare and soften its acceptance.

Never before, in the history of the United States, has there been an ideological camp so fully formed and equipped to extend itself as neoconservatism in the year 1999. It was, and remains, a sect that has some of the properties of a party. There are mentors now in the generation of the fathers as well as the grandfathers, summer internships for young enthusiasts, semiofficial platforms of programmed reactions to breaking news. But to grasp their collective character, one must think of a party that does not run for office at election time. They can therefore evade responsibility for botched policies and the leaders who promote those policies. Donald Rumsfeld had his first and warmest partisans among the neoconservatives, but they were also the first, with the solitary apparent exception of Cheney, to identify him as a scapegoat for the Iraq war and to call for his firing when the insurgency tore that country apart in 2006.

With the peculiar tightness of its loyalties and the convenience of its immunities, neoconservatism in the United States now has something of the consistency of an alternative culture. Its success in penetrating the mainstream culture is evident in the pundit shows on most of the networks and cable TV, and in the columns of the *Washington Post* and the *New York Times*. In the years between 1983 and 1986, and again, more potently, in 2001–2006, the neoconservatives went far to dislocate the boundaries of respectable opinion in America. The idea that wars are to be avoided except in cases of self-defense suffered an eclipse from which it has not yet returned, largely owing to the persistence of respected opinion makers in urging the spread of freedom and markets by force of arms. More particularly, and to confine ourselves to recent events, the nomination to the Supreme Court of Samuel Alito, and the drafting and legitimation of the "surge" strategy by retired general Jack Keane and Frederick Kagan of the AEI, could not have succeeded as they did without the early and organized advocacy of the neoconservative camp.

How did they get so close to Dick Cheney? The answer lies in the fact that Cheney has an inquisitive mind, and yet, from the accidents of his career and placement, he was for a long time a thinker deprived of intellectual society. Neoconservatism, as it developed in the 1980s, came to have its own heroes (Robert Bork), its canon of revered texts (Allan Bloom's *Closing of the American Mind*), and a set of prejudices delivered in a reasonable tone: hostile to individual liberty, appreciative of modern technology, friendly to religion as a guide to morals and an engine of state power. It was, to repeat, a substitute culture of satisfying density.

The AEI along with journals like *Commentary* and, more recently, the *Weekly Standard,* offered, for those who took the full course, a total environment, an idiom of managerial-intellectual judgment that combined the rapidity of journalism with the weightier pretensions of an academy.

In the Washington of the 1980s, the elder Kristols and the Cheneys were rising together, and they became close friends. This alliance easily passed to the younger generation: William Kristol in 2003 boasted to David Carr of the the *New York Times* ("White House Listens When Weekly Speaks") that "Dick Cheney does send over someone to pick up 30 copies of [the *Weekly Standard*] every Monday"—a statement that remains the best clue we have to the number of persons who work for the vice president. The self-confidence of this substitute culture fortified Cheney's sense that he had always already heard the relevant views, and that he had come into contact with the best minds—minds free of the conformist cant and the cost-free sentimentality of modern liberalism.

Cheney's ruling passion appears to be a love of presidential power. Go under the surface a little and this reveals itself as something more mysterious: a restless desire of power after power. It is a quality of the will that seems accidentally tied to an office, a country, or a given system of political arrangements. Jack Goldsmith, the head of the Office of Legal Counsel who fought hard against encroachments on the laws by Cheney and his assistant David Addington, remarked later with consternation and a shade of awe: "Cheney is not subtle, and he has never hidden the ball. The amazing thing is that he does what he says.

Relentlessness is a quality I saw in him and Addington that I never saw before in my life." Yet there is nothing particularly American about Cheney's idea of government, just as there is nothing particularly constitutional about his view of the law; and no more broadly characterizing adjective, such as "Christian," will cover his ideas of right and wrong.

Those who have studied him most closely—James Mann, Charlie Savage, Barton Gellman—agree that his drive to consolidate executive power goes back to one formative experience of seeing men of power checked and denied their prerogatives. As Gerald Ford's chief of staff, he was a witness, close up, to the Church Committee investigations of the mid-1970s. The reforms that followed those investigations would open up rights for citizens against domestic surveillance, and would create the machinery for lawmakers to curb the exuberance and inspect the conduct of the national security apparatus. Among the reforms of the time was FISA—the Foreign Intelligence Surveillance Act—which Cheney deplored as soon as it passed and has sought ever since to circumvent. Here, as elsewhere, Addington may be supposed to give an uncensored glimpse of the vice-president's view: "We're one bomb away from getting rid of that obnoxious court."

Something deep and unspoken in Cheney plainly rebels against the idea that conventional lawmakers, whose only power lies in their numbers, could ever check or by law prevent the actions of a leader vested with great power. He thought Nixon should not have resigned and advised George H. W. Bush not to seek approval from Congress for the first Gulf War. Even at the time of the Church investigations, Cheney made an exception for the chief executive to the Freedom of Information Act, and secreted in a vault the government's "family jewels": findings of an internal investigation that he believed should be a state secret. These papers, declassified by the CIA in June 2007, included evidence of CIA kidnappings, assassination plots, and illegal domestic spying.

He sought and obtained the resignation of William Colby as director of the CIA for too readily cooperating with the Church Committee; but he could also count on some reliable friends in his rebellion. Brent Scowcroft, who wrongly took Cheney to be a moderate, concurred for pragmatic reasons of his own. A more wholehearted ally was a young lawyer from the Nixon justice department, Antonin Scalia. By 1977, one thing was clear to both Cheney's allies and his opponents. He wanted a great deal of power to be held as closely as possible by the president. When he ran for Congress in 1978 and won election for the first of six terms, he got himself quickly appointed to an odd combination of committees: Ethics and Intelligence. They had in common the access they offered to secrets of entirely different kinds.

One of Cheney's first public statements as secretary of defense under George H. W. Bush was a talk at an AEI conference in May 1989, entitled "Congressional Overreaching in Foreign Policy." There, already, he spoke of the "inviolable powers inherent in the presidential office." On the other hand, he saw Congress as a body of "535 individual, separately elected politicians, each of whom seeks to claim credit and avoid blame." A contempt for the readiness to compromise and the want of resoluteness in

Congress as a whole marked Cheney's utterances on the subject from the moment he left Congress.

But some such disdainful view of lawmakers had been implicit a year earlier, in the Iran-Contra minority report, which he released in the closing months of the Reagan administration. Secret operations in Nicaragua in the mid-1980s, undertaken by elements of the National Security Council and the State Department, seemed to Cheney justified by the legitimate powers of the unitary executive. Even though Congress had made a law expressly forbidding those actions, the fault lay with Congress for having meddled in affairs that belonged by right to the president. The US invasion of Panama in December 1989—overseen by Cheney as secretary of defense—was in this sense not only a rehearsal for the first Gulf War but a vindication of Reagan's use of executive power south of the border.

Soon after becoming vice president, Cheney plucked out of obscurity and brought back to government two men, John Poindexter and Elliott Abrams, still under a shadow from having been charged with various crimes in the Iran-Contra prosecutions. Poindexter became the projector of Total Information Awareness—a war-on-terror idea rejected by Congress, which would have encouraged Americans to spy on their neighbors—while Abrams was made an adviser on Middle East policy and then adviser for global democracy strategy. Poindexter would resign in 2003 over the scuttling of his fantastic proposal that the military run an online betting service to reward persons who correctly forecast future terrorist acts, coups, and assassinations. Abrams stayed with Middle East policy and in 2006 secured a declaration of American support for the Israeli bombing and invasion of Lebanon. A zeal that touched the brink of recklessness had always belonged to the public characters of both men.

Yet Cheney had been given carte blanche by George W. Bush to run the transition in 2000–2001: a solitary commander dispensing orders to an obedient crew. Bush was simply not part of this scene. Every member of the first Bush cabinet was approved by Bush, of course, but every one happened to have been Cheney's first choice. (When Paul O'Neill, at Treasury, offered dissident comments on the economic program—including opposition to Bush's tax cuts and Iraq war plans—Cheney thought he should go and Bush without any question agreed.) Yet his control went far deeper. In assessing this administration, one must never forget the advantage bestowed by interlocking circles of previously enjoyed patronage. Not only to Wolfowitz and Libby and Addington had Cheney been a patron—the maker of promotions, for them, long before Bush came on the scene—the same could be said for the person closest of all to the president, his chief of staff Andrew Card.

Meanwhile, to monitor the policymaking at State he had John Bolton and Robert Joseph, while, at Defense, there were Stephen Cambone, Douglas Feith, and later Eric Edelman. Higher up was Rumsfeld: a former superior who became an equal and then—because he was less artful and made himself obnoxious to others as Cheney did not—a subordinate with privileges. Last and easiest to forget, there was Colin Powell: the lately promoted four-star general whom Cheney, in an unprecedented move in 1989, had brought in over the heads of the Pentagon and created as chairman of the Joint Chiefs of Staff. Such favors are never forgotten; and Powell's old debt to Cheney, as much as Cheney's undermining of departmental dissent in the run-up to the war in Iraq, would have inhibited Powell from the honest scrutiny of the plan for war that many expected from a conscientious man in his position.

How far did Cheney's interests and involvement go into the making of policy? He has conceded that he was allowed by his understanding with Bush to participate on some issues while keeping an enforced silence on others. From what Jane Mayer and Barton Gellman report, this appears to have been an understatement of his range. According to Gellman, all things military were Cheney's province; also domestic and foreign policy; natural resources and energy policy; and nominations and appointments. The burden of Jane Mayer's book *The Dark Side* is that the president allowed Cheney—armed with an emergency exception worked up by Addington, John Yoo, and others—to transgress the limits on state action toward American citizens as well as enemy prisoners and unknown persons taken in combat. Bush wanted this job done; but Cheney was the master architect, managing at once the details and the rationale—and Bush signed off. Bush approved, that is, extreme interrogations that included waterboarding (formerly known as the drowning torture); renditions to "black sites" where prisoners are tortured by the police of states known for their brutality; and the creation of a class of stateless persons-without-rights, "enemy combatants," to reside at Guantánamo without protection from American laws or any other laws. The meaning of the Office of the Vice President was that actions were to be meditated and ordered there; in the president's office, they were ratified as accomplished facts, and given the force of law.

Cheney's team did not take no for an answer. The vice president early on impressed Bush with the maxim that negotiation is a form of surrender, and Bush was happy to echo the sentiment: "We're not going to negotiate with ourselves on taxes." But Addington said it straighter: "We're going to push and push and push until some larger force makes us stop." They were seldom met by that force—in the president or the people around him, or among the Democrats in Congress. If anything, the president, by his incidental exhibitions of will, troubled the designs of the Office of the Vice President more than the opposition party. Ahmad Chalabi, for example, was a favorite client of the Cheney circle, and their choice to lead an Iraqi puppet state after the war. He was a fluent and gifted confidence man; but he got on Bush's nerves. "What was Chalabi doing sitting behind Laura last night?" he asked after the 2004 State of the Union. The mass protests led by the Ayatollah Sistani and Bush's irritation at Chalabi combined to turn the administration from the idea of a patriot-dictator to the plan for a constitutional assembly in Iraq.

But the Cheney team has never been stopped for long. The story of the National Security Agency data mining in violation of FISA has a typical shape in this regard. The White House successfully frightened the *New York Times* out of publishing the discovery of this practice for a year after James Risen's story was ready to go. When it did appear, the attorney general, Alberto Gonzales, threatened to prosecute the newspaper. Meanwhile, the head of the

NSA, Michael Hayden, took shelter in a Jesuitical economy of truth, saying that one end of an intercepted "conversation" had to be in a foreign country before a wiretap would cover an American. This was true of phone conversations, but not of the transactional data of phone calls and the numbers, the addresses and subject lines of emails, and so on.

"Government," writes Gellman in *Angler*, "collected information on a scale that potentially touched every American"; and presumably it still does, since in June 2008 Congress handed the president a nerveless compromise allowing minimal oversight of the renewable sweeps of electronic communications. The structure of the intelligence agencies and departments since that scandal has brought them even closer to Cheney. The cooperative attitude of Hayden at the NSA got him a job as head of the CIA; and the new position of director of national intelligence was shifted from John Negroponte to someone more nearly a protégé: John Michael McConnell, a subordinate of Cheney's at Defense in the administration of George H. W. Bush.

About none of these actions has Cheney ever been called, by a subpoena from Congress or an urgent demand from the press, to answer questions regarding the extent and legality of his innovations. It is as if people do not think of asking him. Why not? The reluctance shows a tremendous failure of nerve, from the point of view of democracy and public life. But there is a logic to the sense of futility that inhibits so many citizens who have been turned into spectators. It comes from the dynamic of the co-presidency itself, to which the press has grown acclimatized. Bush is the front man, and is known as such. He takes questions. If he answers them badly, still he is there for us to see. To address

Cheney separately would be to challenge the supremacy of the president—a breach of etiquette that itself supposes a lack of the evidence that would justify the challenge.

The fact that Bush's answers are so inadequate, from a defect of mental sharpness and retentiveness as well as dissimulation, kills the appetite for further questions. But the fact that the questions have, in a formal sense, been asked and answered lets the vice president off the hook. Thus the completeness of his silence and seclusion, for long intervals ever since September 11, 2001, is an aberration that has never been rebuked and has often gone unnoticed. "There is a cloud over the vice-president," said the prosecutor Patrick Fitzgerald in his summation at the trial of Lewis Libby. "That cloud is something you just can't pretend isn't there."

But for much of the second term of the Bush-Cheney administration, we have been pretending. The man who held decisive authority in the White House during the Bush years has so far remained unaccountable for the aggrandizement and abuse of executive power; for the imposition of repressive laws whose contents were barely known by the legislature that passed them; for the instigation of domestic spying without disclosure or oversight; for the dissemination of false evidence to take the country into war; for the design and conduct of what the constitutional framers would have called an *imperium in imperio*, a government within the government.

2

What Went Wrong: The Obama Legacy

June 2015

> A political virtuoso . . . might write a manifesto suggesting a general assembly at which people should decide upon a rebellion, and it would be so carefully worded that even the censor would let it pass. At the meeting itself he would be able to create the impression that his audience had rebelled, after which they would all go quietly home—having spent a very pleasant evening.
>
> —Kierkegaard, *The Present Age*

Any summing-up of the Obama presidency is sure to find a major obstacle in the elusiveness of the man. He has spoken more words, perhaps, than any other president; but to an unusual extent, his words and actions float free of each other. He talks with unnerving ease on both sides of an issue: about the desirability, for example, of continuing large-scale investment in fossil fuels. Anyone who voted twice for Obama and was baffled twice by what followed—there must be millions of us—will feel that this president deserves a kind of criticism he has seldom received. Yet we are held back by an admonitory intuition. His predecessor was worse, and his successor most likely will also be worse.

One of the least controversial things you can say about Barack Obama is that he campaigned better than he has governed. The same might be said about Bill Clinton and George W. Bush, but with Obama the contrast is very marked. Governing has no relish for him. Yet he works hard at his public statements, and he wishes his words to have a large effect. Even before he ascended to the presidency, Obama enjoyed the admiration of diverse audiences, especially within black communities and the media. The presidency afforded the ideal platform for creating a permanent class of listeners.

Winning has always been important to Obama: to win and be known as a winner. (Better, in fact, to withdraw from a worthwhile venture than be seen not to succeed.) Alongside this trait, he has exhibited a peculiar avoidance of the *business* of politics. The pattern was set by the summer of 2009. It came out in the way he shunned the company of his own party, the invitations that didn't issue from the White House, the phone calls that weren't made, the curiosity that never showed. Much of politics is a game, and a party leader must enter into the mood of the game; it is something you either do or don't have an appetite for. Of our recent presidents, only Eisenhower revealed a comparable distaste.

Obama has sometimes talked as if he imagined that, once he moved to the White House, the climb would be in the past. Indeed, some major drawbacks of his first year as president—the slowness in explaining policies and nominating persons to the federal judiciary and other important posts—may be traced to his special understanding of that year's purpose. It was intended as a time for the country to get to know him. According to a tally published by the CBS correspondent Mark Knoller, the twelve months between January 2009 and January 2010 included 411 occasions for speeches, comments, or remarks by Obama, 42 news conferences, and 158 interviews. The theory seemed to be that once the public trust was sealed, persuasion and agreement would follow. Mastery of the levers of government was desirable, of course, but it could be postponed to another day.

Meanwhile, Obama's hesitation in assuming his practical responsibilities was unmistakable; it could be glimpsed at unguarded moments. There was his comment in response to a peevish remark by John McCain during the February 2010 health-care summit, which the president moderated. "Let me just make this point, John," he said, "because we are not campaigning anymore." He meant: there are lots of things that we shouldn't argue about anymore. McCain looked more bewildered than affronted, and his emotion was shared by others who noticed the curt finality of the reply.

Obama meant that the game was over. Now was the time for putting his policies into practice (doubtless with suitable modifications). We had heard enough about those policies during the campaign itself. Postelection, we had left discussion behind and entered the phase of implementation. In the same vein and with the same confidence, he told Republicans on Capitol Hill three days after his inauguration: "You can't just listen to Rush Limbaugh and get things done." But they could, and they did. The Republicans had an appetite for politics in its rawest form; for them, the game had barely begun.

To declare the argument over in the midst of a debate is to confess that you are lacking in resources. This defect, a failure to prepare for attacks and a corresponding timidity in self-defense, showed up in a capital instance in 2009. Obama had vowed to order the closure of the prison at Guantánamo Bay as soon as he became president. He did give the order. But as time passed and the prison didn't close of its own volition, the issue lost a good deal of attraction for him. The lawyer Obama had put in charge of the closure, Greg Craig, was sacked a few months into the job (on the advice, it is said, of Obama's chief of staff, Rahm Emanuel). Guantánamo had turned into baggage the president didn't want to carry into the midterm elections. But the change of stance was not merely politic. For Obama, it seemed, a result that failed to materialize after a command had issued from his pen was sapped of its luster.

Yet as recently as March of 2015, Obama spoke as if the continued existence of the prison were an accident that bore no relation to his own default. "I thought we had enough consensus where we could do it in a more deliberate fashion," he said. "But the politics of it got tough, and people got scared by the rhetoric around it. Once that set in, then the path of least resistance was just to leave it open, even though it's not who we are as a country and it's used by terrorists around the world to help recruit jihadists." One may notice a characteristic evasion built in to the grammar of these sentences. "The politics" (abstract noun) "got tough" (nobody can say why) "and people" (all the people?) "got scared" (by whom and with what inevitability?). Adverse circumstances "set in" (impossible to avoid because impossible to define). In short, once the wrong ideas were planted, the president could scarcely have done otherwise.

The crucial phrase is "the path of least resistance." In March 2015, in the seventh year of his presidency, Barack Obama was presenting himself as a politician who followed the path of least resistance. This is a disturbing confession. It is one thing to know about yourself that in the gravest matters you follow the path of least resistance. It is another thing to say so in public. Obama was affirming that for him there could not possibly be a question of following the path of courageous resistance. He might regret it six years later, but politics set in, and he had to leave Guantánamo open—a symbol of oppression that (by his own account) tarnished the fame of America in the eyes of the world.

It is perhaps understandable that Obama felt a declaration of his intention to close Guantánamo need not be followed by the political work of closing it. For Barack Obama sets great store by words. He understands them as a relevant form of action—almost, at times, a substitute for action. He takes considerable authorial pride in the autobiography he published before becoming a politician. We may accordingly ask what impression his spoken words have made in his presidency, from the significant sample we now possess.

He employs a correct and literate diction (compared with George W. Bush) and is a polite and careful talker (compared with Bill Clinton), but by the standard of our national politics Obama is uncomfortable and seldom better than competent in the absence of a script. His show of deliberation often comes across as halting. His explanations lack fluency, detail, and momentum. Take away the script and the suspicion arises that he would rather not be onstage. The exception proves the rule: Obama has a fondness for ceremonial occasions where the gracious quip or the ironic aside may be the order of the day, and he is deft at handling them. As for his mastery in delivering a rehearsed speech, the predecessor he most nearly resembles is Ronald Reagan.

This presents another puzzle. Obama said during the 2008 primaries that he admired Reagan for his ability to change the mood of the country—the ability itself, he meant, abstracted from the actual change Reagan brought. Astonishingly, Obama seems to have believed, on entering the White House, that his power as an interpreter of the American Dream was on the order of Reagan's. But this ambition was less exorbitant than it looked; the differences between their certitudes are small and cosmetic. Reagan spoke of the "shining city on a hill." Obama says: "I believe in American exceptionalism with every fiber of my being."

He came into office under the pressure of the financial collapse and the public disenchantment with the conduct of the Bush-Cheney "war on terror." It has been said that this was an impossible point of departure for our first black president. Might the opposite be true? The possibilities were large because the breakthrough was unheard-of. The country was exhausted by eight years on a crooked path. The nature of the doubt, the nature of the uncertainty, it is possible to think, made the early months of 2009 one of those plastic hours of history when the door to a large transformation swings open. Obama himself evidently saw it that way. On June 3, 2008, having just won the Democratic primaries, he declared in Minnesota that people would look back and say, "This was the moment when the rise of the oceans began to slow, and our planet began to heal." The language was messianic, but the perception of a crisis and of the opportunity it offered was true.

Obama's warmest defenders have insisted, against the weight of his own words, that such hopes were absurd and unreal—often giving as evidence some such conversation stopper as "this is a center-right country" or "the American people are racist." But the same American people elected an African American whose campaign had been center-left. He inherited a majority in both houses of Congress. It takes a refined sense of impossibility to argue that Obama in his first two years actually traveled the length of what was possible.

During Obama's first year in office, the string of departures from his own stated policy showed the want of connection between his promises and his preparation to lead. The weakness was built in to the rapid rise that carried him from his late twenties through his early forties. His appreciative, dazzled, and grateful mentors always took the word for the deed. They made the allowance because he cut a brilliant figure. Obama's ascent was achieved too easily to be answerable for the requirement of performing much. This held true in law school, where he was elected president of the *Harvard Law Review* without an article to his name, and again in his three terms as an Illinois state senator, where he logged an uncommonly high proportion of noncommittal "present" votes rather than "ayes" or "nays." Careless journalists have assumed that his time of real commitment goes further back, to his three years as a community organizer in Chicago. But even in that role, Obama was averse to conflict. He was never observed at a scene of disorder, and he had no enemies among the people of importance in the city.

He came to the presidency, then, without having made a notable sacrifice for his views. Difficulty, however—the kind of difficulty Obama steered clear of—can be a sound instructor. Stake out a lonely position and it sharpens the outline of your beliefs. When the action that backs the words is revealed with all its imperfections, the sacrifice will tell the audience something definite and interesting about the actor himself. Barack Obama entered the presidency as an unformed actor in politics.

In responding to the opportunities of his first years in office, Obama displayed the political equivalent of dead nerve endings. When the news broke in March 2009 that executives in AIG's financial-products division would be receiving huge bonuses while the federal government paid to keep the insurance firm afloat, Obama condemned the bonuses. He also summoned to the White House the CEOs of thirteen big banks. "My administration," Obama told them, as Ron Suskind reported in *Confidence Men*, "is the only thing between you and the pitchforks." But the president went on to say that "I'm not out there to go after you. I'm protecting you." Obama was signaling that he had no intention of asking them for any dramatic sacrifice. After an embarrassed reconsideration, he announced several months later that he had no use for "fat cats." But even that safe-sounding disclaimer was turned upside down by his pride in his acquaintance with Lloyd Blankfein, of Goldman Sachs, and Jamie Dimon, of JPMorgan Chase: "I know both those guys; they are very savvy businessmen." His attempt to correct the abuses of Wall Street by bringing Wall Street into the White House might have passed for prudence if the correctives had been more radical and been explained with a surer touch. But it was Obama's choice to put Lawrence Summers at the head of his economic team.

In foreign policy, Afghanistan was the first order of business in Obama's presidency. His options must have appeared exceedingly narrow. During the campaign, he had followed a middle path on America's wars. He said that Iraq was the wrong war and that Afghanistan was the right one: Bush's error had been to take his eye off the deeper danger. By early spring of 2009, Obama knew that his judgment—though it earned him praise from the media—had simply been wrong. The US effort in Afghanistan was a shambles, and nobody without a vested interest in the war was saying otherwise.

Two incidents might have been seized on by a leader with an eye for a political opening. The first arrived in the form of diplomatic cables sent to the State Department in early November 2009 by Karl W. Eikenberry, the ambassador to Afghanistan and, before that, the senior commander of US forces there. Eikenberry's length of service and battlefield experience made him a more widely trusted witness on Afghanistan than General David Petraeus; his cables said that the war could not be won outside the parts of the country already held by US forces. No more troops ought to be added. Eikenberry recommended, instead, the appointment of a commission to investigate the state of the country. Any reasonably adroit politician would have made use of these documents and this moment. With a more-in-sorrow explanation, such a leader could have announced that the findings, from our most reliable observer on the ground, compelled a reappraisal altogether different from the policy that had been anticipated in 2008. Though Obama had his secretary of state, Hillary Clinton; his secretary of defense, Robert Gates; and the chairman of the Joint Chiefs of Staff, Michael Mullen, arrayed against him, he also had opponents of escalation, including Vice President Biden and others, at the heart of his policy team. He chose to do nothing with the cables. A lifeline was tossed to him and he treated it as an embarrassment.

A plainer opportunity came with the killing of Osama bin Laden on May 2, 2011. This operation was the president's own decision, according to the available accounts, and it must be said that many things about the killing were dubious. It gambled a further erosion of trust with Pakistan, and looked to give a merely symbolic lift to the American mood, since bin Laden was no longer of much importance in the running of al-Qaeda: the terrorist organization was atomized into a hundred splinter groups in a dozen countries. The temporary boost to patriotic morale that came from this spectacular revenge may also have influenced Americans to accept more casually the legitimacy of assassinations.

That he killed the instigator of the September 11 attacks surely helped Obama to win reelection in 2012. With a larger good in view, he might also and very plausibly have used the death of bin Laden as an occasion for ending the occupation of Afghanistan. If the Eikenberry cables afforded a chance to tell the unpopular truth no politician wants to utter—"We can't win the war"—the death of bin Laden offered a prime opportunity to recite a comforting fiction to the same effect: "Al-Qaeda is our enemy. It is now a greatly diminished force, and we have killed its leader. At last, after so much pain and sacrifice, we can begin to wind down the war on terror."

But Obama made no such gesture. He held on to his December 2009 plan, which had called for an immediate escalation in Afghanistan to be followed by de-escalation on a clock arbitrarily set eighteen months in advance. The days after the killing saw the White House inflating and deflating its accounts of what happened in Abbottabad, while Obama himself paid a visit to SEAL Team Six. A truth about the uses of time in politics—as Machiavelli taught indelibly—is that the occasion for turning fortune your way is unlikely to occur on schedule. The delay in withdrawing from Afghanistan was decisive and fatal, and it is now a certainty that we will have a substantial military presence in that country at the end of Obama's second term.

꜠ •• ꜡

Much of the disarray in foreign policy was inevitable once Obama resolved that his would be a "team of rivals." The phrase comes from the title of Doris Kearns Goodwin's book about the Civil War cabinet headed by President Lincoln. To a suggestible reader, the team-of-rivals conceit might be taken to imply that Lincoln presided in the role of moderator; that he listened without prejudice to the radical William Seward, his secretary of state, and the conservative Montgomery Blair, his postmaster general; that he heard them debate the finer points of strategy and adjudicated between them. Actually, however, Goodwin's book tells a traditional (and true) story of Lincoln as a *leader*, both inside the cabinet and out.

The idea of a team of rivals stuck in Obama's mind because it suited his temperament. But the cabinet he formed in 2009 involved a far more drastic accommodation than any precedent can explain. Obama hoped to disarm all criticism preemptively. He had run against Hillary Clinton—who did lasting damage by saying that he was unqualified to lead in a time of emergency—and he paid her back by putting her in charge of the emergency. For the rest, Obama selected persons of conventional views, largely opposed to his own and in some cases opposed to one another. It was an unorganized team, perhaps not a team at all, but that hardly mattered. The cabinet met nineteen times during his first term, an average of only once every eleven weeks.

The largest issues on which Obama won the Democratic nomination were his opposition to the Iraq war and his stand against warrantless domestic spying. He had vowed to filibuster any legislation giving immunity to telecommunications companies, and withdrew that pledge (with a vow to keep his eye on the issue) only after he secured the nomination. And yet among all the names in the cabinet there was not one opponent of warrantless surveillance on his domestic team, and, on his foreign-policy team, no one except Obama himself who had spoken out or voted against the Iraq war. (Lincoln, by contrast, placed abolitionists in two critical posts: Seward at State and Salmon Chase at Treasury.) Thus, on all the relevant issues, Obama stood alone; or rather, he would have stood alone if his views had remained steady. His choice not only of cabinet members but of two chief advisers—Summers and Emanuel—could be read as a confession that he was intimidated in advance.

Obama's foreign policy also revealed a trait he shares with most other Democratic presidents: he considers domestic policy his major responsibility. Foreign policy is a necessary encumbrance; it is a burden to be transferred to other hands. What Democrats have never properly recognized is that for any powerful and expanding state, foreign entanglements set definite limits on what is possible at home. The energy and expenditure that went into wars such as Korea, Vietnam, Afghanistan, and Iraq had broad consequences for domestic benefits as various as social insurance and environmental protection.

Obama's domestic policy has, for the most part, exhibited a pattern of intimation, postponement, and retreat. The president and his handlers like to call it deliberation. A fairer word would be "dissociation." Once Obama walks out of a policy discussion, he does not coordinate and does not collaborate. This fact is attested by so many in Congress that it will take a separate history to chronicle the disconnections. He intensely dislikes the rituals of keeping company with lesser lawmakers, even in his own party. Starting with the Affordable Care Act, he has stayed aloof from negotiations, as if recusing himself afforded a certain protection against being blamed for failure. He does not cultivate political friends, or fraternize with comrades. Add to this record his episodic evacuations of causes (global warming between 2010 and 2012; nuclear proliferation between 2011 and 2015) and the activists who got him the nomination in 2008 may be pardoned for wondering what cause Obama ever espoused in earnest.

One of the surprises of reviewing the conception and execution of the Affordable Care Act is that Obama came to the subject late and almost experimentally. In the 2008 primaries, the health-care policies of Hillary Clinton and John Edwards were widely judged to be more comprehensive than Obama's, and he would later concede he had been wrong to reject the individual mandate. But in the earliest days of the new administration, he tested the popularity of two quite different investments of political capital: health care and climate change. Health care won out. He delegated the responsibility for drafting the measure to five separate committees of Congress and sent his vice president to run interference for many months. No serious speech was given to explain the policy, and how could there be a speech? There wasn't yet a policy. In the meantime, he suspended engagement with most of the other issues that might be judged important. Between

January 2009 and March 2010, health care swallowed everything. Obama did it because he wanted to "do big things," to have a piece of "signature legislation."

If he was a cautious president-elect in November 2008, he seemed to be in full retreat by the end of 2010. A few days after the midterm disaster, Obama vowed to carry forward the Bush tax cuts for the richest Americans. When the Republican majority saw weakness so clearly telegraphed, their threat to close the government and their refusal to raise the debt ceiling in 2011 were foreseeable obstructions. The president, for his part—as Harry Reid's chief of staff observed with genuine shock—had no Plan B. Eventually, Obama spun out an improbable compromise. He met the Republican ultimatum with an offer of sequestration of government funds, which would enforce across-the-board budget cuts in the absence of a later deal. This measure was extorted by panic. Obama apparently assumed that the drawbacks in funding for education, food inspection, highway construction, and other essential activities of government would be immediately evident to the American public. It has proved an empty hope. Sequestration will be part of the Obama legacy as much as the Affordable Care Act.

When the Tea Party sprang up in reaction to the Troubled Asset Relief Program and the ACA, Obama never mentioned the protest and never sought to challenge the movement. Through his first term he barely recognized its existence. Only when pressed would he name the Tea Party, but even then he spoke of the threat to his policies in a vague generic way: the Tea Party represented an age-old tendency in American politics, founded on innocent misunderstanding. There was nothing to be done about it.

This strain of quietism has been a recurrent and uneasy motif of Obama's presidency. But the trait is deeply rooted. How else to explain his avoidance of meetings with Kathleen Sebelius in the run-up to the launch of the ACA's insurance exchanges? That a busy president might not ask for a weekly progress report in the year preceding the rollout is understandable. But considering how much the result mattered—not just to his legacy but also to the trust in government he had pledged to restore—what could be the excuse for conversing face-to-face with the secretary of health and human services only once in the three and a half years before the unveiling? The new law is bringing medical care to millions who never before could rely on such protection. In the long run, it is likely to be a tremendous benefit to the society at large. Yet opposition to the reform has never let up.

Given the weight of the moment, it was extraordinarily careless of the president to have allowed its effect to be diluted by a succession of avoidable delays. He also missed the opportunity to supply a single conclusive explanation of the meaning of his reform. Along with his contradictory declarations on Syria, the botched health-care rollout did more than anything else to spoil the first year of Obama's second term. It scuttled any chance the Democrats may have had for preserving their Senate majority.

Different as the issues have been, Obama's retreat from controversy in dealing with Guantánamo, his deference to the generals in Afghanistan even when circumstances took his side, and his willingness to cede health care to a complex bureaucratic machine that lacked any competent controls all shared a characteristic signature. His resort to the path of least resistance has been a consistent and almost reflexive response to friendly conditions that turn suddenly hostile. But the hostility in question may be something more than partisan suspicion and rancor.

It now seems clear that during the presidential transition, between November 2008 and January 2009, Obama was effectively drilled in the intricacies of US operations abroad, the secret deployment of special forces, the expansion of domestic spying by the NSA, and the full extent of terror threats both inside and outside the United States (as determined by the high officials of the security apparatus). More than could have been expected from a principled politician, he was set back on his heels. It would be understandable if he was also frightened.

The first visible effect of his re-education was the speech he gave at the National Archives on May 21, 2009. Whatever might become of Guantánamo itself, the policy Obama laid down at the National Archives ensured that the United States would maintain a category of enemy combatants charged with no specific crime. These prisoners would be as helpless as those whom Bush and Cheney had "rendered" or sent to Guantánamo. The speech defined a category of permanent detainees—their cases impossible to try in court, because the evidence against them had been obtained by torture; their condition now irremediable, because they posed a continuing threat to the United States.

Obama also followed Cheney's path in keeping much of the war on terror off the books by employing mercenaries—known now by the euphemism "contractors." He held on to another Cheney innovation when he invoked the state-secrets privilege to undercut legal claims by prisoners seeking redress and citizens invoking the Fourth Amendment protection against searches and seizures. Privilege of this kind is not compatible with the functional necessities of a constitutional democracy.

The right to a fair and speedy trial is guaranteed by the Constitution, as are all the conditions for a relevantly informed discussion of public affairs. In the Obama administration, however, as in the Bush-Cheney administration before it, the war on terror was to stand on a different footing. Matters relating to war and domestic security were closed to the scrutiny of the people. The shift in Obama's attitude between April and June 2009 could not have been more conspicuous. He delivered the National Archives speech in response to many weeks of harsh and testing attacks by the Republican right, and especially by Cheney, who denounced the decision by the new president to publish the torture memos and a second series of Abu Ghraib photographs. When Obama surrendered on these fronts, they knew they had him on the run in Guantánamo, Afghanistan, and elsewhere.

Obama's expansion of the war on terror was predictable, but at every stage he raised people's hopes before dashing them. He made waterboarding illegal, together with many other practices of "enhanced interrogation." This was a brave achievement to which no minus sign can be attached. At the same time, he brought John Brennan into the White House to organize command procedures for drone killings. In the manner of Cheney, Obama kept secret the document establishing the legal rationale for the strikes. By the end of 2014, Obama had ordered 456 drone attacks (compared with 52 by Bush). Unhappily, there is truth in the charge by Bush's supporters that President Obama has spared himself the illegality of torture by killing the suspects whom his predecessor would have kidnapped for "enhanced interrogation."

In foreign policy across the greater Middle East, Obama's major concern was to avoid any suggestion of a religious war against Islam. His speech in Cairo on June 4, 2009, was the first step in that direction. His plan to negotiate a State of Palestine was supposed to be the second. In the drawn-out confusion of the Arab Spring, however, he allowed himself to be trapped by the combination of neoconservative advocates of never-ending war, such as Robert Kagan, and liberal believers in humanitarian war, such as Samantha Power and Anne-Marie Slaughter, whose claim to a "responsibility to protect" licensed NATO's bombing of Libya and the overthrow of Muammar Qaddafi. Obama's decision to follow their advice has brought anarchy to Libya and made it a depot for jihadists in the region.

The scale of the Libyan disaster was already known when the same advisers and opinion makers knocked on Obama's door for intervention in Syria. Once again, he had a hard time resisting, and was almost lured into a major bombing attack and an attempt at the overthrow of Bashar al-Assad. Only much later would Obama acknowledge that it was "a fantasy" that the United States could outflank the Islamist rebels by subsidizing an American-vetted moderate force, "essentially an opposition made up of former doctors, farmers, pharmacists and so forth." The worst feature of the engagements in Libya and Syria has been the president's refusal of honest explanations to the public. In Libya, this refusal was accompanied by something approaching a denial of responsibility. He has referred most questions regarding Libya to Hillary Clinton's State Department, but Obama was the president. He approved the no-fly interdiction that shaded into the destruction of a government and wrought a civil war. If the chaos that ensued has added to the horrors of the sectarian conflict in the region, part of the fault lies with Obama. In both Syria and Iraq, a necessary ally in the fight against Sunni fanatics (including the recent incorporation that calls itself the Islamic State) has been the Shiite regime in Iran. Yet Obama has been hampered from explaining this necessity by his extreme and programmatic reticence on the subject of Iran generally.

About the time the last sentence was written, President Obama announced the framework of a nuclear deal between the P5+1 powers and Iran. If he can clear the treaty with Congress and end the state of all but military hostility that has prevailed for nearly four decades between the United States and Iran, the result will stand beside health care as a second major achievement. To bring it off will demand tremendous resourcefulness and a patience as unusual as the impetus that drove the Affordable Care Act. And it will require even greater strength of resolution. An uncompromising personal investment will have to be shown, and will have to persist against fierce opposition. Obama will have to recognize that his most dedicated opponents—the neoconservatives who dictate Republican foreign policy—are relentless and that they will go on until they are stopped.

Nevertheless, a lasting détente with Iran seems possible; what are the obstacles?

Until this moment, Obama has taken care not to disturb the American consensus that Iran is a uniquely dangerous country. He has said and done little to counter the right-wing Israeli propaganda that pictures Iran as the greatest exporter of terrorism in the world. His peace-bearing Ramadan messages to non-fanatical believers in Islam have eluded notice in the American press and made no impact on public opinion. The arrogance of his executive action on Libya, too, left a residual irritation that can now be exploited to throw a cloak of principle over merely partisan or expedient opposition to the nuclear deal. These obstacles can only be resisted by the constant pressure of argument that gives reasons and tirelessly repeats its reasons. A president whose main talent has seemed to be inspiration, not explanation, will have to venture now, very far and very often, into the field of lucid explanation. But Obama today has Europe backing him; and elements of the Israeli intelligence community show signs of breaking away from Netanyahu's insistence on the posture of war. The result may depend ultimately on the willingness of a few well-placed senators to part with an old enemy whose status has become familiar and almost customary.

A forgotten aspect of the current nuclear negotiations is that they had a precursor. The agreement that Obama hopes to secure was anticipated and turned down by the president himself in May 2010. At that time Turkey and Brazil had offered to receive low-enriched uranium from Iran in return for allowable nuclear fuel and the opening of trade and lifting of sanctions. Why Obama spurned the offer, as Trita Parsi related in *A Single Roll of the Dice*, remains something of a mystery. It may have been ill suited to domestic politics on the way to a midterm election; and the deal had not been properly coordinated with Russia. Perhaps, too, there was an element of pique: credit for the breakthrough would have been stolen from the American president by two upstart minor powers. Mrs. Clinton also played a significant part in deflecting the Brazil-Turkey proposal.

When such incidents add up to a critical mass, they can no longer be taken as accidents. They tell us something discouraging about the Obama White House and its relation to the State Department. The shortest description of the disorder is that President Obama does not seem to control his foreign policy. A recent and dangerous instance, still unfolding in Ukraine, began in November 2013 and reached its climax in the February 2014 coup that overturned the Yanukovych government. But the coup in Kiev was only the last stage of a decade-long policy of "democracy promotion" that looked to detach Ukraine from Russia. Victoria Nuland, the assistant secretary of state for European and Eurasian affairs, boasted in December 2013 that the United States had spent $5 billion since 1991 in the attempt to convert Ukraine into a Western asset. The later stages of the enterprise called for constant deprecation of Vladimir Putin, which went into high gear with the 2014 Sochi Olympics and has not yet abated. When Nuland appeared in Kiev to hand out cookies to the anti-Russian protesters, it was as if a Russian operative had arrived to cheer a mass of anti-American protesters in Baja California.

Through the many months of assisted usurpation, no word of reprimand ever issued from President Obama. An intercepted phone call in which Nuland and Geoffrey Pyatt, the ambassador to Ukraine, could be heard picking the leaders of the government they aimed to install after the coup, aroused no scandal in the American press. But what could Obama have been thinking? Was he remotely aware of the implications of the crisis—a crisis that plunged Ukraine into a civil war and splintered US diplomacy with Russia in a way that nothing in Obama's history could lead one to think he wished for? His subsequent statements on the matter have all been delivered in a sedative nudge-language that speaks of measures to *change the behavior* of a greedy rival power. As in Libya, the evasion of responsibility has been hard to explain. It almost looks as if a cell of the State Department assumed the management of Ukraine policy and the president was helpless to alter their design.

Suppose something of this sort in fact occurred. How new a development would that be? Five months into Obama's first term, a coup was effected in Honduras with American approval. A lawyer for the businessmen who engineered the coup was the former Clinton special counsel Lanny Davis. Did Obama know about the Honduras coup and endorse it? The answer can only be that he should have known; and yet (as with Ukraine) it seems strange to imagine that he actually approved. It is possible that an echo of both Honduras and Ukraine may be discerned in a recent White House statement enforcing sanctions against certain citizens of Venezuela. The complaint, bizarre on the face of it, is that Venezuela has become an "unusual and extraordinary threat" to the national security of the United

States. These latest sanctions look like a correction of the president's independent success at rapprochement with Cuba—a correction administered by forces inside the government itself that are hostile to the White House's change of course. Could it be that the coup in Ukraine, on the same pattern, served as a rebuke to Obama's inaction in Syria? Any progress toward peaceful relations, and away from aggrandizement and hostilities, seems to be countered by a reverse movement, often in the same region, sometimes in the same country. Yet both movements are eventually backed by the president.

The situation is obscure. Obama's diffidence in the face of actions by the State Department (of which he seems half-aware, or to learn of only after the fact) may suggest that we are seeing again the syndrome that led to the National Archives speech and the decision to escalate the Afghanistan war. Edward Snowden, in an interview published in the *Nation* in November 2014, seems to have identified the pattern. "The Obama Administration," he said, "almost appears as though it is afraid of the intelligence community. They're afraid of death by a thousand cuts . . . leaks and things like that." John Brennan gave substance to this surmise when he told Charlie Rose recently that the new president, in 2009, "did not have a good deal of experience" in national security, but now "he has gone to school and understands the complexities." This is not the tone of a public servant talking about his superior. It is the tone of a schoolmaster describing an obedient pupil.

However one reads the evidence, there can be no doubt that Obama's stance toward the NSA, the CIA, and the intelligence community at large has been the most feckless and unaccountable element of his presidency. Indeed, his gradual adoption of so much of Cheney's design for a state of permanent emergency should prompt us to reconsider the importance of the deep state—an entity that is real but difficult to define, about which the writings of James Risen, Mike Lofgren, Dana Priest, William Arkin, Michael Glennon, and others have warned us over the past several years. There is a sense—commonly felt but rarely reflected upon by the American public—in which at critical moments a figure like John Brennan or Victoria Nuland may matter more than the president himself. There could be no surer confirmation of that fact than the frequent inconsequence of the president's words, or, to put it another way, the embarrassing frequency with which his words are contradicted by subsequent events.

Bureaucracy, by its nature, is impersonal. It lacks an easily traceable collective will. But when a bureaucracy has grown big enough, the sum of its actions may obstruct any attempt by an individual, no matter how powerful and well placed, to counteract its overall drift. The size of our security state may be roughly gauged by the 854,000 Americans who enjoy top-secret security clearances, according to the estimate published by Priest and Arkin in the *Washington Post* in 2010. The same authors reported that nearly 2,000 private companies and 1,300 government organizations were employed in the fields of counterterrorism, intelligence gathering, mass surveillance, and homeland security.

When Obama entered the White House, it was imperative for him to rid the system of the people who would work against him. Often they would be people far back in the layers of the bureaucracy; and where removal or transfer was impossible, he had to watch them carefully. But in his first six years, there was no sign of an initiative by Obama to reduce the powers that were likeliest to thwart his projects from inside the government. On the contrary, his presumption seems to have been that all the disparate forces of our political moment would flow through him, and that the most discordant tendencies would be improved and elevated by this contact as they continued on their way.

One ought to say the best one can for a presidency that has created its own obstacles but has also been beset by difficulties no one could have anticipated. Obama has governed in a manner that is moderate-minded and expedient. He has been mostly free of the vengeful and petty motives that can derail even a consummate political actor. His administration, the most secretive since that of Richard Nixon, has been the reverse of transparent, but it has also been entirely free of political scandal. There is a melancholy undercurrent to his presidency that recalls Melville's lines in "The Conflict of Convictions": "I know a wind in purpose strong—/ It spins *against* the way it drives."

Though Obama has hardly been a leader strong in purpose, his policies have indeed spun against the way they drove. Nobody bent on mere manipulation would so often and compulsively utter a wish for things he could not carry out. Yet Obama has done little to counteract the regression of constitutional democracy that began with the security policies and the wars of Bush and Cheney. This degeneration has been assisted under his negligent watch, sometimes with his connivance, occasionally by exertions of executive power that he has innovated. Much as one would like to admire a leader so good at showing that he means well, and so earnest in projecting the good intentions of his country as the equivalent of his own, it would be a false consolation to pretend that the years of the Obama presidency have not been a large lost chance.

3

Act One, Scene One

February 2017

What to make of him? The man is a shock, like the toy buzzer in a prank handshake, and the effect is to baffle and immobilize thought. Consider a typical reaction from the morning after the election, Aaron Sorkin's rant on the *Vanity Fair* website: "The Klan won last night. White nationalists. Sexists, racists and buffoons . . . misogynistic shitheads everywhere . . . If he does manage to be a douche nozzle without breaking the law for four years, we'll make it through those four years." Or consider the message read out to vice president–elect Mike Pence by the cast of *Hamilton* after he attended a performance: "We are the diverse America who are alarmed and anxious that your new administration will not protect us, our planet, our children, our parents, or defend us and uphold our inalienable rights, sir. But we truly hope that our show has inspired you to uphold our American values and to work on behalf of all of us." This has at least the value of staking a claim to decency in language that is decent; but the hopeful words of the performers of *Hamilton* and the flailing words of the creator of *The West Wing* betray the same stunned bewilderment.

By the first week of December, it was hard to recall the mood of a few weeks earlier—a mood in which it had been possible for Noah Feldman, a Harvard law professor, to write a column for *Bloomberg* entitled "On November 9, Let's Forget Donald Trump Happened." In 2003, six years out of law school, Feldman drafted the constitution for the Coalition Provisional Authority in Iraq, and his confidence in the future of Iraqi democracy was now equaled by his confidence in a Hillary Clinton victory. Afterward, he wrote, we should "treat Trump voters as though the whole sorry episode of his candidacy never occurred." Aglow with triumphal assurance and magnanimity, he added this reservation: "Patronizing Trump voters would also be a mistake—practically, rather than morally. The risk of condescension is especially great." On November 9 the risk of condescension (or gloating) had changed sides in a way no well-appointed liberal could have guessed.

The sporadic protests that followed the election were a response to a generalized threat, not a particular grievance; but the shock to the laws and institutions of the country could already be felt in Trump's first three days as president. The Trans-Pacific Partnership was repudiated, and a few hours later Trump ordered the construction of the promised wall with Mexico; an absolute ban was issued on immigration from seven Islamic countries, and a warning given to American "sanctuary cities": if they refused to cooperate with plans for the detention of undocumented immigrants, they would lose federal funding. The process of repealing Obamacare was launched, all mention of climate change was scrubbed from the White House and State Department websites, and Trump signed executive orders to reopen the Keystone XL and the Dakota Access oil pipelines. His pre-inaugural negotiations to reclaim American jobs—particularly at a Carrier factory in Indiana that produces air conditioners, but with similar reverse migrations at Ford and Boeing—were a timely piece of political cunning and showmanship. His thank-you tour and the roughly 30,000 jobs he can claim to have brought back were strategically placed in the swing states that clinched his majority in the electoral college.

In *Leviathan* Hobbes said that what we call the "deliberation" of the will is nothing but "the last appetite, or aversion, immediately adhering to" an action. Whatever the general truth of the analysis, Trump's process of thought works like that. If Obama often seemed an image of deliberation without appetite, Trump has always been the reverse. For him, there is no time to linger: from the first thought to the first motion is a matter of seconds; the last aversion or appetite triggers the jump to the deed. And if along the way he speaks false words? Well, words are of limited consequence. What people want is a spectacle; they will attend to what you do, not what you say; and to the extent that words themselves are a spectacle, they add to the show. The great thing about words, Trump believes, is that they are disposable. Among the prodigies of 2016 was the lightness with which he slipped out of his association with the "birther" movement that had questioned Obama's status as a US citizen: "I was wrong," he said, and that was that.

(He added, for the hell of it, that Mrs. Clinton had been a birther before him: a lie and easily exposed, but forgotten as soon as uttered.)

Neoliberals have spent a quarter of a century arranging the ingredients for the catastrophe. Lenin said of Stalin that "this cook will give us peppery dishes," and for all the talk of nation-building, democracy promotion, multicultural-ism, and tribal recognition, globalization à la NATO has been a peppery dish. There were several chefs involved: Bill and Hillary Clinton, George W. Bush, Barack Obama, and their exemplar Tony Blair. They all wanted to convert the populace to an enlightened internationalism, but along the way they forgot to talk us out of nationalism. The military operations that dismantled Yugoslavia and overthrew the undemocratic governments of those artificial entities Iraq and Libya were meant to be an earnest of the goodwill of the global improvers. The trouble is that wars tend to reinforce nationalism, and unnecessary wars, where the fighting is drawn out and the result chaotic, leave people doubtful and suspicious. Trump, on the campaign trail, said he had always stood against America's Middle Eastern wars, which he blamed on Bush as much as Obama. This was shown to be a wishful self-revision, but he had been laying plans for longer than most people realized. Six days after Obama's victory in 2012, he filed a trademark applica-tion for the phrase "Make America Great Again" and he was soon tweeting that the election was illegitimate and urging his followers to join the revolution. But Trump has always acted as a destabilizer-at-large more than a propounder of doctrine, and the majority of votes for him in 2016 were votes to stop talking about the world, start doing things for America, and bring back our jobs. By late October, the surest sign of his resilience was the fizzle and thud after a decade-old tape of his dirty talk was leaked. The Clinton people thought it would finish him. When the sparks flew but no fire ignited—Michelle Obama said she had never heard talk like that and the right blogosphere dug up some ugly Jay-Z lyrics and linked to Jay-Z's invitation to the Obama White House—there was no telling what might happen next.

Postelection, the liberal argument veered away from Trump and turned to the important question of whom to blame. The initial target was the director of the FBI, James Comey, who in July had refused to indict Mrs. Clinton, but criticized her use of an insecure email server while she was secretary of state. A few days before the election, Comey gave notice of another possible violation only to clear her again. A more popular and reliable target was Vladimir Putin, the preferred enemy on the horizon for neoconservatives, adepts of humanitarian war, and the national security state as far back as the Sochi Olympics. It is possible that Trump's defiance of this multifarious establishment actually helped his popularity with non-political voters. Damage more telling than any emanation from the FBI or Russia probably came from Hillary Clinton's remark that half of Trump's supporters were "a basket of deplorables"—an unforced error that was rightly read as an expression of contempt, addressed to her audience at the LGBT for Hillary Gala held at Cipriani Wall Street, and overheard by undecided voters in Michigan, Wisconsin, and Pennsylvania.

With the election and partial legitimation of Trump against the massed energy of the Democratic Party, many Republicans, and virtually all the mainstream media, we have witnessed a revolution of manners. Will a political revolution follow? What is ominous is the uncertainty and the leaderless state of the opposition. The Democrats are at their lowest ebb since 1920, and this is anything but a sudden misfortune: the loss of nerve started with the election of Ronald Reagan in 1980, which surprised the Democrats and shook their confidence in the tenability of the welfare state; and the threat to mixed constitutional government was clear in the 1994 midterm election, when 367 Republican candidates signed the Contract with America, with its pledge to slash government spending in the first hundred days of a new Congress. The contract was the precursor of the Tea Party; its instigator, Newt Gingrich, has become a leading adviser to Donald Trump. The Democrats behaved persistently as if the Republican hostility to government-as-such were a curable aberration. Yet eight years of Obama have ended with his party's loss of the presidency, its relegation to a minority in both houses of Congress, and—something that happened when no one was counting—the loss of 900 seats in state legislatures. Any return to majority status must begin at the local and state levels, yet in the fifty states of the union, the Republican Party has thirty-three governors and now controls thirty-two legislatures. The losses grew steeper with every mishap, from the delay of the Affordable Care Act in 2009 to the standoff over the national debt ceiling in the summer of 2011. Yet after Obama's re-election, as the PBS Frontline documentary *Divided States of America* vividly recalled, he thought he was in 2008 again, the old mandate renewed, and would say to reporters in 2012 and 2014 just as he had done in 2010: "the [Republican] fever will break."

Trump's inaugural address carried the stamp of hot ambition even in its salutation: "Chief Justice Roberts, President Carter, President Clinton, President Bush, President Obama, fellow Americans and people of the world, thank you." What were the people of the world doing here? It has been conjectured that Trump was greeting a blood-brotherhood of the *popolari* that encompassed the followers of Farage, Le Pen, Orbán, Wilders, and others. Just as likely, given the grandiosity of the man, he meant to suggest that the fate of the world was so implicated in his ascension that it was only polite to say hello. The next section, however, seemed to see the American people as deciders for the world: "We, the citizens of America, are now joined in a great national effort to rebuild our country and restore its promise for all of our people. Together, we will determine the course of America and the world for many, many years to come." This was immediately followed by an attempt to divide friend from enemy within the United States. Against me, the establishment ("Washington"); with me, the people—or rather the people who matter. In the new era of globalization, "politicians prospered but the jobs left and the factories closed. The establishment protected itself, but not the citizens of our country. Their victories have not been your victories. Their triumphs have not been your triumphs." For the people, for once, this inauguration day would be a day of celebration, and Trump would rejoice with them: "January 20th, 2017 will be remembered as the day the people became the rulers of this nation again. The forgotten men and women of our country will be forgotten no longer."

These men and women had been noticed before: they were the "silent majority" invoked by Richard Nixon. The speechwriter who coined that phrase, Pat Buchanan, would become the insurgent Republican of the 1992 primaries, and at the 1992 party convention he gave a speech that seems the prototype for Trump's inaugural. In fact, Trump delivered no passage as inflammatory as Buchanan's "there is a religious war going on in our country for the soul of America. It is a cultural war"; and he issued no call to battle comparable with Buchanan's peroration: as the US army in the riots of that year "took back the streets of LA, block by block, so we must take back our cities, and take back our culture, and take back our country." Trump's speech was in the same key, but far more diffuse and less provocative.

"We are one nation," he said, speaking of the forgotten people, "and their pain is our pain. Their dreams are our dreams, and their success will be our success. We share one heart, one home and one glorious destiny." But if we really believe this, we cannot go on subsidizing other nations through alliances, foreign aid, and military interventions while "America's infrastructure has fallen into disrepair and decay." Even as Bush and Obama chased a distant foe in Afghanistan and Iraq, "one by one, the factories shuttered and left our shores." If "their pain is our pain" was a Bill Clinton touch, the use of "shuttered" evoked Obama's early speeches on the need for jobs—Trump's speechwriters are indisputably eclectic. When he went on to speak of "rusted-out factories scattered like tombstones across the landscape of our nation" and "the crime and gangs and drugs that have stolen too many lives and robbed our country of so much unrealized potential," liberal commentators accused him of dark hyperbole, and certainly the picture was overdrawn. But Trump was calling on a resentment caused by quite recent events. After the exporter of jobs and General Electric CEO Jeffrey Immelt entered the White House as its jobs tsar, in 2011, Obama switched definitively to a cooler upbeat tone and "the economy" took the place of "jobs." Trump knows what a letdown this was. Accordingly, he passed from the dank image of shuttered and rusted factories, crime-ridden neighborhoods, and children ruined by drugs to an emotionally satisfying and opportunistic climax: "This American carnage stops right here and right now." The diktat—the stress on immediate action—made clear once again the authoritarian quality of the man, and the sentence "Now arrives the hour of action" sounded as if it was translated from German. (But then, Obama said in September 2009 "Now is the season for action"—different, but how exactly?)

Trump vowed to enact tariffs and enforce trade protection. He would "bring back our borders" and "unite the civilized world against radical Islamic terrorism"—Fox radio hosts have long charged Obama with harboring occult reasons for never saying the words "Islamic terrorism" though he has always spoken plainly against "terror," "terrorism," and "acts of terror." Trump also added his personal assurance—in the "protector" protocol innovated by Bush and ratified by Obama—that he would guarantee the safety of the American people. "There should be no fear. We are protected, and we will always be protected." As if to say to a child: the night is dark and dangerous but I am with you. After a routine summons to self-sacrifice— "whether we are black or brown or white, we all bleed the same red blood of patriots"—he unleashed the maxim that will guide his policy:

> From this day forward, it's going to be only America first, America first. Every decision on trade, on taxes, on immigration, on foreign affairs will be made to benefit American workers and American families ... We will seek friendship and goodwill with the nations of the world, but we do so with the understanding that it is the right of all nations to put their own interests first.

His adoption of the phrase "America first" was made a cause of scandalized rebuke by people who know that the spokesman for the original America First movement, seventy-seven years ago, was Charles Lindbergh, an anti-Semite who warmly sympathized with Hitler's politics. (How many of these people also know that John F. Kennedy was an early supporter of America First?) But the underlying question was not whether Trump was giving a secret signal to anti-Semites—among his biggest supporters are the prime minister of Israel and the mayor of Jerusalem—but rather what he means by putting our own interests first. He said America would not seek "to impose our way of life on anyone," which seems a clear warning against nation-building such as Bush and Obama attempted in Afghanistan. Yet the tone of the speech and the tone of the man leave us uncertain whether our interests are best served by peace or war; and in an administration bristling with generals as well as oligarchs, an aggressive platitude about the virtue of our way of life scarcely settles the question. An anti-Muslim alarmist and advocate of multiple wars like Frank Gaffney can think that Trump is on his side. So, with as much reason, can an anti-interventionist like Buchanan. Events will not allow Trump to profit much longer from this calculated ambiguity. Besides, the deeper danger of his populism, as Jan-Werner Müller remarked in "Capitalism in One Family," is that a leader who sets up as spokesman for the "real people" inevitably sows violent division. The other people, the unreal ones, are pictured as tools or puppet-masters, the glitter and the rot. Trump is likely to feel no scruple about hardening this contrast.

Obama was a softener of the truth, congenitally averse to blunt statement or calling things by their shortest names. Trump is an incorrigible liar. When, for example, he wanted to justify his decision to exempt Christians from his ban on immigrants from Syria, he said on January 27 on the Christian Broadcasting Network that he was merely executing a correction to the law under Obama, when "if you were a Muslim you could come in, but if you were a Christian, it was almost impossible." That statement, if made by anyone else, we could call a flat-out lie. In Trump, it is a lie that belongs to a peculiar pathology, an exceptional grammar. You cite a "fact" that you calculate will draw opinion to your side; you do this partly because it fits with other things you heard somewhere and you expect not to be contradicted because you say a lot of things like that, and most of them never catch up with you, dog your steps, and compel a denial; but if the statement is proved false, through and through, beyond the possibility of denial and without a single person of consequence to support you, when at last a concession is required you blame it on the failure of the circulation of facts in the world.

How often will he be caught at it? The national security state that Obama inherited and broadened, and has now passed on to Trump, is so thoroughly protected by secrecy that on most occasions concealment will be an available alternative to lying. Components of the Obama legacy that Trump will draw on include the curtailment of the habeas corpus rights of prisoners in the war on terror; the creation of a legal category of permanent detainees who are judged at once impossible to put on trial and too dangerous to release; the expanded use of the state secrets privilege to deny legal process to abused prisoners; the denial of legal standing to American citizens who contest warrantless searches and seizures; the allocation of billions of dollars by the Department of Homeland Security to supply state and local police with helicopters, heavy artillery, state-of-the-art surveillance equipment, and armored vehicles; precedent for the violent overthrow of a sovereign government without consultation and approval by Congress (as in Libya); precedent for the subsidy, training and provision of arms to foreign rebel forces to procure the overthrow of a sovereign government without consultation and approval by Congress (as in Syria); the prosecution of domestic whistleblowers as enemy agents under the Foreign Espionage Act of 1917; the use of executive authority to order the assassination of persons—including US citizens—who by secret process have been determined to pose an imminent threat to American interests at home or abroad; the executive approval given to a nuclear modernization program, at an estimated cost of $1 trillion, to streamline, adapt, and miniaturize nuclear weapons for up-to-date practical use; the increased availability—when requested of the NSA by any of the other sixteen US intelligence agencies—of private internet and phone data on foreign persons or US citizens under suspicion. The last of these is the latest iteration of Executive Order 12333, originally issued by Ronald Reagan in 1981. It had made its way through the Obama administration over many deliberate months, and was announced only on January 12. As with the nuclear modernization program in the realm of foreign policy, Executive Order 12333 will have an impact on the experience of civil society that Americans have hardly begun to contemplate. Obama's awareness of this frightening legacy accounts for the unpredictable urgency with which he campaigned for Hillary Clinton—an almost unseemly display of partisan energy by a sitting president. All along, he was expecting a chosen successor to "dial back" the security state Cheney and Bush had created and he himself normalized.

How did America pass so quickly from Obama to Trump? The glib left-wing answer, that the country is deeply racist, is half-true but explains too much and too little. This racist country voted for Obama twice. A fairer explanation might go back to the financial collapse of 2008 when Americans had a general fear and were shocked by what the banks and financial firms had done to us. "In an atmosphere primed for a populist backlash," John Judis observed in August 2010, Obama "allowed the right to define the terms." The revolt of 2008–2009 was against the financial community and anyone in cahoots with them, but the new president declined to name a villain: when he invited thirteen CEOs to the White House in April 2009, he began by saying he was the only thing standing between them and the pitchforks, and ended by reassuring them that they would all work together. No culprit would be named and no sacrifice called for. Trump emerged early as an impresario of the anger, a plutocrat leading the people's revolt against plutocracy. The most credible explanation for the popular turn to the right—there are plenty of examples of people who voted twice for Obama but then for Trump—was offered by the Italian legal scholar Ugo Mattei. As he sees it, the resemblances between Trump and Berlusconi run deep, and in both cases the appeal derives from popular cynicism more than credulity. The voters have come to understand that the big banks, along with investment companies like Goldman Sachs and transnational corporations, are sovereignties as powerful as states and in some cases more powerful. By vesting a billionaire with extraordinary power, therefore, the voters are going straight to the relevant authority and cutting out the middleman—the politician.

Trump unquestionably shares this perception with the people who voted for him. In a radio interview in 2015, he recalled his visit to Russia in 2013, in an unsuccessful attempt to close a deal on apartment complexes. "I was with the top-level people," he said, "both oligarchs and generals, and top of the government people . . . I met the top people, and the relationship was extraordinary." Though it may seem a tiny slip, one notices the distinction between top-level people and the top people in government. Oligarchs and generals come first and rank highest in

Trump's estimation; top government people are worth knowing, but secondary. Trump likes the relationship of money to power in Russia—and specifically of financial power to government authority—more than he admires anything special about Putin, whom he has never met and about whom he knows little. Evidence of a vaguer affinity can be tracked in his appointment of four billionaires and three generals to senior advisory or cabinet positions: in his US government the "top-level people" will be identical with the "top of the government people." By comparison, Obama, like the younger Bush and Bill Clinton, delegated authority for projects like the Trans-Pacific Partnership to quasi-political mediators who could work with financial bigwigs because they also came from that environment. Peter Orszag, Lawrence Summers, Timothy Geithner, William Daley, Michael Froman, Jason Furman, and Jack Lew were all finance-to-government mediators of this stamp. Trump, however, gives up all pretense of a distinction between finance and government. A possible reaction is delight, as at an honest revelation. A later reaction may be fury, as at a betrayal.

But money is something most people feel they can understand, with the right guidance. Government seems much harder. If you want to know the reason, listen to Obama, in one of the many postelection interviews he granted, responding to a question about the degree of his surprise at the election result:

I think all of us, and that includes the campaign, felt that there were certain thresholds with respect to somebody becoming president that during the course of the campaign President-elect Trump had not crossed, and I think there was probably some sense internally that because he had not run a traditional campaign or behaved in a traditional way, despite the success that he had shown, that at the end of the day he would not inspire enough overperformance in any sector that it would throw off the data as much as it did.

This slurred and heavy-lifting patois is typical of Obama off script, and the mix of corporate and technocratic jargon and media cliché will defeat any reader's first attempt to parse the sense. Now listen to Trump on Twitter:

> Someone incorrectly stated that the phrase "DRAIN THE SWAMP" was no longer being used by me. Actually, we will always be trying to DTS.
>
> I met some really great Air Force GENERALS and Navy ADMIRALS today, talking about airplane capability and pricing. Very impressive people!
>
> Yes, it is true—Carlos Slim, the great businessman from Mexico, called me about getting together for a meeting. We met, HE IS A GREAT GUY!

He is the loudmouth at the bar, cocksure and full of himself and you may want him to stop, but you catch his drift. Trump is short-winded, vulgar, and lowbrow, where Obama was long-winded, refined, and impeccably middlebrow.

Trump's most disturbing habit is also his most ridiculous trait: he credits and is apt to repeat his professed beliefs when—and in exact proportion as—he sees other people credit them. We normally think of beliefs as something you cannot choose (unlike opinions or estimations), but Trump does choose and he correlates the numbers of his followers with truth in the physical world. So when, in an interview on January 25, the ABC reporter David Muir inquired into his unsubstantiated belief that between three and five million people voted illegally, accounting for Hillary Clinton's popular majority, Trump replied: "You know what's important? Millions of people agree with me when I say that." The when-I-say-that is essential to Trump's belief and essential to the relationship to his beliefs enjoyed by millions. His belief, triggered by impulsive attraction to something dressed as a fact, is fortified against refutation by the echo of the belief from his followers. The pride of a demagogue is never quite compatible with sanity; and none of Trump's actions has so perplexed the media and dismayed his party as his ordering of an investigation into possible illegalities in the election that delivered Republican control over all three branches of government.

As for the oligarchs and generals, it is hard to say which is the most unqualified or inappropriate. James Mattis, Michael Flynn, and John Kelly, the generals appointed as secretary of defense, national security adviser, and secretary of homeland security, are all renowned as haters of Iran, though Mattis has said he will abide by the nuclear deal. Kelly thinks a border wall with Mexico will be insufficient: we need "a layered defense" with protection extending "1500 miles south" of the Texas border and involving agreements with Peru. The richest of the billionaires appears to be Trump's nominee for secretary of education, Betsy DeVos, a promoter of charter schools who has shown considerable disdain for public schools. Tom Price, the doctor who is the nominee for health secretary, owes his appointment to his agitation for the repeal of Obamacare. Andrew Puzder, the CEO of the fast-food franchise Carl's Jr., chiefly known for his opposition to raising the minimum wage, is Trump's pick for labor secretary.

The most ominous appointment for the laws and liberty of the country is the new director of the Central Intelligence Agency, Mike Pompeo. A former representative from Kansas, Pompeo has cited Obama's revision of Executive Order 12333 as providing legal support for the expanded surveillance of US citizens. Under his directorship, Pompeo conceded, the rights of an American citizen will be "considered in assessing whether it is lawful to target the individual," but that sounds a good deal like the "process" Obama and his drone czar John Brennan claimed to employ when looking at the targets of drone-fired missiles in Pakistan, Iraq, and elsewhere. There was a process, all right, even in cases where the personal identity of the target was unknown, but it was never what anyone could call due process. Pompeo, in a speech to a church group in Kansas three years ago, spoke of the war on terror as a religious war and said that Americans must "pray and stand and fight and make sure that we know that Jesus Christ our savior is truly the only solution for our world." Fourteen Democrats voted with the Senate majority to confirm him as the new director of the CIA, including Dianne Feinstein, the former vice chairman of the Senate Select Committee on Intelligence and the ranking Democrat on the Senate Judiciary Committee, and the new Senate minority leader, Chuck Schumer. This would have been an excellent opportunity for a minority leader to signal the propriety of opposition, but Feinstein's capitulation was stranger still, in view of Pompeo's outright advocacy of torture: she had demonstrated great persistence and courage during Obama's second term in extracting from the CIA the congressional oversight report on torture and securing from a reluctant White House the permission to publish its summary. Pompeo condemned that torture investigation as "quintessentially at odds with duty to country."

When, in early January, the directors of the FBI, the CIA, and National Intelligence combined to issue a report on the alleged Russian hacking of the election and went some way to implicate Trump, their intervention could have been taken for an effort to precipitate a constitutional crisis. The report offered conclusions without the evidence to back them up; seldom has so foggy a document been treated with such respect by mainstream journalists; and the partial abstention of the NSA—which endorsed the conclusions with only "moderate" confidence—made the situation even more obscure. Now that Trump is president, impeachment affords the only opening for an early shove out the door. A constitutional footing might be found in the foreign emoluments clause (Article I, Section 9, Clause 8) and the application is plain enough. Trump Hotel in Washington is not yet divested, and stands to profit enormously when foreign dignitaries stay there to curry favor with the world's new boss: "no Person holding any Office of Profit or Trust under [the United States], shall, without the Consent of the Congress, accept of any present, Emolument, Office, or Title, of any kind whatever, from any King, Prince, or foreign State." The Democrats, however, have for a generation been hesitant to act as accusers in any merely political context. They may routinely charge Republicans with sexism or racism, but constitutional illegalities they regard as tedious and extracurricular. At the height of the reaction against Cheney and Bush in 2007, when their violation of the Foreign Intelligence Surveillance Act was at the center of national discussion, the Democratic majority leader in Congress, Nancy Pelosi, announced that impeachment was "off the table." That is something a politician in her position might well think but should not say; it typifies the Democratic Party's continuing state of mind and etiquette.

As soon as the 2016 election result came in, Americans on the popular left began throwing about the word "resistance." The right of resistance comes into play (according to Locke and Jefferson) when a previously legitimate government breaks its compact with the people. This justification has seldom, if ever, been used against an elected government before it took office. But a larger confusion was apparent here, one that responsible politicians who saw that Trump was unqualified should have taken an interest in clearing up. There is a marked difference between resistance and opposition. Resistance is in order when a person's civic conscience forbids obedience to laws introduced and enforced by a criminal government. Opposition ought to be more common: in a constitutional system it has an indispensable function when one party dominates unscrupulously and the opposing party works to prevent the damage that would be done by adoption of the majority party's policies. An opposing party of substance can also use what power it has to articulate with precision the miscarriages of authority it detects in the conduct of the majority; and it can be expected to vote against a person nominated to high office whose recorded words and actions show him to lack the necessary stature.

There has not been a time in the past half-century when Americans stood so much in need of a political opposition. It is early to say this for sure, and Schumer, Pelosi, and other party leaders may discover the resolve they have yet to show, but if the Democrats cannot be roused, another party will have to collect itself for the work of opposition. The summer disorders of 2016 that trod the brink of riots, with their explicit anti-police slogans, simmered down by September and were only a background subject in the presidential debates, but they had much to do with the Republican votes in places like Pennsylvania and Michigan. Apparently unorganized and leaderless protests have gathered about them a certain romantic glamour ever since the Occupy movement of 2011–2012, and yet the real utility of such protests is to serve as a warning when planned in alliance with an existing party. The only other purpose they can have is to initiate a revolution; and people who act from such a motive had better have a chance of succeeding. On the other hand, refusal to obey unjust laws, if carried out by a large enough mass of the people, may crystallize an opposition when party leaders have lost their way.

Democrats have forgotten what it means to constitute an opposition. In the age of Clinton, Bush, and Obama, the presidency was all. Even if the party lost majorities in one or both houses, executive orders and the veto were thought to be as good as laws, or as good as we should expect. The talents of the party know better—senators like Sherrod Brown and Sheldon Whitehouse, Elizabeth Warren and

Chris Murphy—but many others appear not to realize how much they have surrendered. "A majority," Lincoln said in his first inaugural address, "held in restraint by constitutional checks and limitations, and always changing easily with deliberate changes of popular opinions and sentiments, is the only true sovereign of a free people. Whoever rejects it does of necessity fly to anarchy or to despotism." Are Americans a free people by this standard? The most recent changes in popular opinion have been anything but deliberate. We are not yet close to anarchy or despotism, but the checks and limitations will require constant guarding and frequent use in the months to come.

Trump achieved a majority in the electoral college but fell three million short in the popular vote. The nationalist ideology that drove his campaign belongs as yet to a minority. Even so, Trump in his first ten days has already broken through the restraint of familiar constitutional checks and limitations: the duty to abide by the result of elections no matter how they turn out, and the right of religious toleration. Other transgressions are likely to follow at a dizzying pace. The women's marches on the day after the inauguration, with millions of protesters worldwide, were a preventive demonstration against an anticipated evil; but the ban on Muslim immigration is no longer the name of a wrong to be feared. The change is with us, it has happened. And the exemptions from the ban awarded to citizens of America's regional allies of convenience—Egypt, Qatar, the UAE, Pakistan, and Saudi Arabia, the same Saudi Arabia that supplied fifteen of the nineteen hijackers on September 11, 2001—rendered unmistakable the opportunistic character of the act. When Muslims with legitimate visas are stopped from boarding planes to the United States, our freedom of religion in America has become a freedom that *was*. It will remain so until political opposition and organized protest succeed in overturning this ban. The depth of the crisis was confirmed on January 30 when Trump fired Sally Yates, the acting attorney general, who had refused to defend his immigration order. In the preceding days he had purged most of the senior officials of the State Department and given a permanent seat on the National Security Council to his political strategist, Steve Bannon. At the start of February who will say that the alarm felt by so many on November 8 was exaggerated? The entertainment of the autumn, when a would-be Caesar held us fast in our seats by mixing forbidden truths with his lies, has already glutted the heartiest appetite, but the exits are closed and we are still in the first scene of the first act.

4

The Age of Detesting Trump

July 2017

"Putin Butts In to Claim There Were No Secrets, and Says He'll Prove It"—so ran the main headline in the *New York Times* on May 18. The subject was Donald Trump's supposed revelation of foreign intelligence assets when he met with Russian officials in the Oval Office. It isn't yet clear if anything dangerous was done, but the US media were showcasing their heavy artillery with a leak of their own, which had to have come from the White House staff or intelligence agents on the scene. Mostly, however, the article seemed to be an excuse to deploy the expression "Putin Butts In"—a cut below the diction once permitted in the *Times*. This descent into brashness, which teeters on the brink of open contempt, has been a feature of American media coverage of Trump ever since January; it is growing shriller and more indiscriminate, working up to a presumptive climax no one has imagined with clarity. Impeachment is the constitutional name for the fast finale they are hoping for; the idea is that the brass and cymbals will soon enter, lawyers and good spies, private detectives and who knows what else—and out the door goes Trump.

The center-left media went to sleep after the Iran-Contra scandal of 1986–1987, dozed through the Clinton years, and were half-asleep and nodding when they approved Cheney and Bush's war in Iraq and Obama and Hillary Clinton's war in Libya. For obscure reasons, they have been quite certain that Western dismantling of yet another Arab country, Syria, is the surest path to a sane policy in the Middle East. All the mainstream outlets, with CNN and the *Times* at their head, have now re-emerged as anti-government centers of news, opinion, and news perceptibly mingled with opinion. But they are new to the work of "resistance" and it shows. The *Times* on May 27 ran a lead story by Maggie Haberman, Mark Mazzetti, and Matt Apuzzo, headlined in diminishing type: "Kushner Is Said to Have Mulled Russia Channel—Trump Tower Meeting—Aim Was a Secret Means for Communications During Transition." Those lines say all that the story has to say—the channel was never established. But they strung it out to seven short paragraphs based on a leak from "three people with knowledge of the discussion." Fourteen more paragraphs followed rehearsing the likely, possible, or conjectured relations between Trump's associates and various Russians, weaving in the name of Kushner as an intermittent reminder. The *Times* speculation was prompted by an earlier report in the *Washington Post*: Kushner wanted special Russian facilities to prevent intrusion by US intelligence, in order to conduct transitional discussions with

Russia. A strategic misfire on Kushner's part; but no less questionable was the assumption guiding the story: any plan for back-channel privacy is properly viewed as an attempt to dodge the civic duty of all Americans to submit to US surveillance. Now that we know what we know about Putin, nobody *should* be free of surveillance: not the president or his advisers or his cabinet; and surely not members of Congress, either. And federal or state judges, and ordinary citizens—why not? The age of detesting Trump is the age of reliance on the deep state and trust in the "intelligence community." If they can't save us, who will? They need all the powers they have been given if they are to achieve what they must.

On May 29, the *Times* published another front-page Kushner story, this one by Glenn Thrush, Maggie Haberman, and Sharon LaFraniere. The attack now began at the beginning—"The most successful deal of Jared Kushner's short and consequential career in real estate and politics involves one highly leveraged acquisition: a pair of adjoining offices a few penny-loafer paces from his father-in-law's desk in the White House"—and went on to identify Kushner as a "princeling" who has seen "his foothold on that invaluable real estate shrink amid revelations that he has faced new scrutiny." Then things got personal: "his preppy aesthetic, sotto-voce style," his "preference for backstage maneuvering," an "unfailing self-regard," and the way "he quickly forms fixed opinions about people, sometimes based on scant evidence" (no evidence was given for this opinion about Kushner's opinions: no evidence and no source). "He also has a habit," unnamed sources were allowed to dictate once more, "of disappearing during crises." In "Journalism in America," an essay on the flash reporting of the 1920s, H. L. Mencken observed:

> There are times and occasions when rumor is almost as important as the truth—when a newspaper's duty to its readers requires it to tell them not only what has happened, but also what is reported, what is threatened, what is merely said. What I contend is simply that such quasi-news, such half-baked and still dubious news, should be printed for exactly what it is—that it ought to be clearly differentiated from news that, by an over-whelming probability, is true.

The unhappy pattern anyway is starting to be noticed. The *Times* published a sharp letter to the editor a few days later that noticed how the paper had now crossed the line separating news analysis from invective.

This has happened across the board, in the culture of the Trump presidency: you see it in the newspapers, the magazines, and television. Mainstream media are speaking almost in unison; they are out of control with a consistency that shows they have forgotten what control feels like. PEN, for example, now runs a Daily Alert on Rights and Expression. A typical stream of headlines on May 1—under the subheading "PEN America's take on today's most press-ing threats to free expression"—included such items as "The night Donald Trump failed to break the White House correspondents' dinner": "While Donald Trump was in Pennsylvania holding a campaign-style rally, Washington DC celebrated a night of journalism without him. The White House correspondents' dinner gave each guest a

'First Amendment' pin, while Samantha Bee's 'Not the White House Correspondents' Dinner' praised the work of local newspapers." Such was the alert from the US branch of a major international anti-censorship institution. Four weeks earlier, PEN announced that its annual Freedom of Expression Courage Award, which went to *Charlie Hebdo* in 2015, would be given in 2017 to the two million persons who participated in the women's march against Trump.

President Trump, monster and scapegoat, is too rash in his overall demeanor, too uncalibrated in his words and gestures, too ill-adapted to the routines of politics to carry credit even when he is speaking common sense. The Democrats tossed his idea that better relations with Russia "would not be a bad thing" into the general stew of his repulsive ideas on taxes and immigration, and Republicans ignored it as an indigestible ingredient. For now, as Senator Dianne Feinstein of the Senate Intelligence Committee has acknowledged, there is no evidence to support the view that his attitude to Russia is part of a conspiracy that implicates him in Russian hacking of the 2016 election. That there are links between Trump and his real-estate friends and the Russian oligarchs is extremely likely: oligarchs of all nations, but Russia in particular, are the movers in that market, and Trump's credit on Wall Street ran out long ago. Russian money is probably behind some of his precarious loans; and the Russian government keeps track of Russian money. But the US media, and a great many Democrats with them, have been running far ahead of the game and treating the connection as a certainty that ought to assure the collapse of the Trump administration in the near future.

‿ •• ⁀

The firing of the FBI director James Comey was the event that brought suspicions to a pitch that will be hard to maintain, and equally hard to scale down. Much of the provocation came from the multiple explanations offered by Trump. Comey was fired, he said at first, because of his mishandling of the Clinton email investigation; but he had only fired him because his deputy attorney general and attorney general had advised him to; but they were not the efficient cause after all, since he, Trump, had grown dissatisfied with Comey's "showboating"; and more important, as was well known, Comey was incompetent and the Bureau under his leadership a total mess. Folded into each alternative explanation was the assumption that Comey was *not* fired because of the Russia investigation, along with a curious mention of the director's reassurance that Trump was not personally under investigation. Three days after the sacking, Trump tweeted a threat to Comey in gangster grammar: he better hope their conversations were not taped. A final example of the monkeying around that many people think should seal Trump's fate occurred when he invited the Russian foreign minister, Sergey Lavrov, to the Oval Office. Trump barred the White House press corps (but not the Russian media) and told Lavrov that since he had sacked Comey, the Russia investigation was at last off his back. The sequence—you do need the whole sequence—is typical of Trump. He can't walk a straight line, even on a pattern he has rehearsed, without a ballet step in the middle that strikes him as clever in the moment. Thus he undermines the presentation; and something else has to be tried in a hurry.

Trump won election to the highest office in the US government by heaping contempt on government. In this,

he confirmed and strengthened a tendency of the party he
ran with, going back as far as the Reagan administration.
The Democrats by contrast remain the party of what-
government-can-do-for-you; and a substantial mass of their
rank and file denies his legitimacy. He stole the election,
they say; it was handed to him by Comey, or by Putin, or
by an electoral college whose numbers have no right to
cancel the votes of a majority of three million people. The
trick, Democrats feel, is somehow to delegitimate Trump
and the government he leads (it isn't a real government) and
then move in to take his place, but with a government that
has somehow been relegitimated. Apart from the Republican
Freedom Caucus blocking Trump's first modifications of
Obamacare and the push by the neoconservatives McCain
and Graham for some assertion of US military strength
against Russia, there has been almost no sign among
Republicans of any deviation from an opportunistic solidar-
ity with the president. The Republicans own both houses of
Congress as well as the presidency and the Supreme Court.
In this situation, on the way to delegitimating Trump the
Democrats would have to renounce their own allegiance to
constitutional democracy.

The clearest statements on Russian interference, from an
authority known for telling the truth (and having some
relevant truths to tell), were heard in James Comey's testimony before the Senate Intelligence Committee on June 8.
"It was an active measures campaign," he said, "driven from
the top of that government." The eruption was startling and
unmistakable: "It is not a close call. That happened. That is
about as unfake as you can possibly get." Nor did he feign a
seemly doubt about why he was sacked: "I was fired because

of the Russia investigation," and "the endeavor was to change the way the Russia investigation was being conducted." Comey's repeated assurance to Trump that he was not "personally" under investigation—something he confirmed at the hearing—depended on a legalism that could mar an otherwise convincing indictment. He mentioned that one of the seven or eight FBI leaders he spoke with had objected to the usage, because while technically true, it gave a false impression. In this respect the Jesuitical emphasis—Trump was not *personally* under investigation—resembled the assurance given in the public media by intelligence leaders (and by Comey in particular while he was still FBI director) to the effect that it was flatly false that Obama had ever ordered a wiretap of Trump. Again, the point was technically true. But the apparent honesty of the assurance took advantage of a careless anachronism in Trump's language: wiretaps ordered on individuals belong to the espionage of fifty years ago. Obama, of course, didn't order a wiretap of Trump by name, but the Trump campaign, including Trump Tower facilities, was under NSA surveillance; that would have included Trump, and it would have included phones: Obama could know this by deduction even if he wasn't directly informed. Since the intelligence services are part of the executive branch, he could have been shown, or have asked to see, the evidence on Trump at any time. A similar pretense is kept up across a surprisingly wide range of mainstream reports—"surprisingly" if you consider the recentness of the Snowden revelations. The CNN reporter Wolf Blitzer thought it only decent to show some bewilderment when Senator Rand Paul said, in an interview in mid-June, that Trump may well have been spied on and that he thought himself under surveillance too. We know, if we can bear to think it, that everyone is surveilled: that was the meaning of the Prism and XKeyscore programs. Obama never renounced them, nor has Trump. They are there for use or abuse on the part of the executive branch.

Two circumstances favor the conclusion the squadrons of Trump's accusers are driving at: namely, that he knows particular things about the connections between himself, his campaign, and Russian interests which he wants to hide because they place him in legal and political jeopardy. The first is his firing of three people in the justice system who were known to have had a long immersion in Trump-related data: Preet Bharara, the US attorney for the Southern District of New York, who had once been assured by Trump that he could keep his job; the acting US attorney general, Sally Yates; and Comey. The second is the schedule of the last two terminations. On December 29, Trump's nominee as national security adviser, Michael Flynn, spoke on the phone with the Russian ambassador, Sergey Kislyak, about the possibility of sanctions relief for Russia. On January 26, Yates informed the White House counsel Don McGahn that Flynn was in legal jeopardy and had made statements "we knew not to be the truth." (Among other things he had lied to the vice president about never having consulted with Russians.) McGahn summoned Yates back on January 27 and wondered why it mattered to "DOJ if one White House official lies to another." "It wouldn't really be fair of us," Yates replied, "to tell you this and then expect you to sit on your hands." McGahn then asked to see the evidence; Yates said she would see about getting permission. It was on the same day, January 27, that, quite suddenly, Trump called up Comey and invited him to have dinner at the White House: the dinner at which he would ask the FBI director if he could count on his loyalty, and would receive a tactical reply, stressing honesty rather than loyalty. On January 30, Yates called McGahn back to tell him he could "come over and review the underlying evidence." In her testimony before the Senate Intelligence Committee—a presentation extraordinary for its clarity and probity—she added that she never knew if he came, because that was her last day in office; she was fired by Trump on January 30, the ostensible reason being her refusal to enforce his anti-Muslim immigration order.

It has been reported that February 9 was the day Vice President Pence first heard that Flynn had lied about speaking with Kislyak. On February 13, Flynn resigned, and the day after Trump asked his attorney general, his adviser Jared Kushner, and others to leave the room so that he could talk to Comey alone. "I hope you can see your way clear to letting this go, to letting Flynn go," Trump said. "He is a good guy. I hope you can let this go." An odd, almost extracurricular point that draws attention only when you think about it, was Trump's telling Comey that he didn't mind if some of his satellites were casualties in the Russia investigation. Trump, in short, was willing for his associates to be exposed and punished, if it would get the Russia business off his back. During Comey's testimony this was taken by Senator James Lankford, a Republican from Oklahoma, as a likely expression of Trump's belief in his own innocence, and his law-abiding readiness to expose the guilty—an interpretation Comey went along with. But the unexpected emphasis—it's OK for you to arrest my satellites—could as well have been a signal: "I don't mind your taking anyone else as a scapegoat, so long as you leave me in the clear."

There is much more than nothing here. And the legal-investigative team put together by Robert Mueller, the former FBI director and now special counsel appointed to investigate Russian interference, includes lawyers with formidable competence in the scrutiny of money laundering and "financial forensics" generally. A certain doubt persists, largely because despite the long series of tantalizing hints, so far little has come of all the fuss. The lack of evidence on Trump himself is puzzling after the strenuous emphasis of Obama's CIA director, John Brennan; this looks like another sign that impeachment is not something to count on. "Foreign emoluments" is the most plausible charge, but the phrase has a distant sound and one of the words will need explaining. And yet, the idea of a left-liberal-engineered overthrow of Trump, assisted by the intelligence community and lawyers of great genius, has a tremendous, unquenchable charm for the media. Rachel Maddow, the MSNBC news host, leans forward and upward five nights a week in near euphoria at the prospect of the next unwill-ing witness, the next Trump associate, the next recovered document or "new development" that will bring us one step closer to putting this president in handcuffs and shackles.

They may pin their hopes on the intelligence community and eventually the lawyers, but what will maintain the balance of the state in the meantime? The answer that

seems agreed on by moderates of both parties is: the generals. And this is assented to even by a large fraction of the
"resistance" media—on what evidence it would be hard to
say. Americans in the past few months have come to speak
in terms of the most extravagant trust and gratitude about
the presence in the Trump administration of the secretary
of defense, General James Mattis. He is said to have been a
responsible commander with a steady temper; and no
doubt these are welcome traits in the vicinity of Trump.
He is also the general who led the second siege of Fallujah,
the most destructive battle of the Iraq war; and he directed
the exoneration of almost all the Marines who committed
the worst recorded atrocity of that war, the Haditha
Massacre. Trump's delegation of authority to the generals
for deciding all particulars of hostile engagements in Syria
and Iraq may mark the first time such a thing has been
done in US history; it is certainly the first time it has been
admitted in public; and it goes against the spirit of constitutional checks and limitations. Whatever the fancy
bookkeeping of Bush and Obama (turning on such words
as "authorization" and "international norms"), the United
States today is not legally at war with any country, and
generals are understood to make local decisions regarding
foreign policy only when commanding an army against a
declared wartime enemy.

The compulsion to convict Trump of something definite,
something dire, even if not yet a criminal offense, reached a
sort of climax on June 25 when an entire back page of the
Times' Sunday Week in Review was transformed into an
enormous zero-shaped pattern entitled "Trump's Lies,"

under the byline of two reporters, David Leonhardt and Stuart A. Thompson. The dates of more than a hundred "lies" were printed in boldface, the text of the lie in quotation marks and the correction in parenthesis. Most of the lies, however, were what anyone would call opportunistic half-truths, scattershot promises, changes of tack with a denial that any change had taken place, and, above all, hyperbolic exaggerations. Trump uses words like "tremendous" and numbers like "hundreds" or "thousands" in a way that evacuates them of all meaning, but this belongs to the category of rhetorical twisting and pulling in which all politicians indulge. His daft attempt to inflate the size of the crowd at his inaugural seemed an example of reality denial, but it becomes a lie, fairly so-called, when measured against his slander of those who conveyed the verifiable truth. Again, his statement that "we're the highest-taxed nation" was part of a spew, false and meant as a hyperbolic version of "our taxes are too high," a sort of statement that exacerbates (and panders to) the usual indifference to details among his followers: a bad thing in a president. But the *Times* article laid much stress on doubtful instances such as Trump saying that Obama had wiretapped him or that "the story that there was collusion between the Russians & Trump campaign was fabricated by Dems as an excuse for losing the election." He is mostly right, there, even if the word "fabricated" is wrong; there had been no official notice about collusion until Comey's announcement before the intelligence committee on March 20; before that, it was a widespread rationalization of defeat by the Democrats. And though the circumstantial links between Trump associates and Russia show that the story was not fabricated out of thin air, convincing evidence, to repeat, has not yet been made public.

"Putin derangement syndrome," as the *Rolling Stone* journalist Matt Taibbi called it, has entered the culture with the irresistibility of a fast-spreading rash. The *Late Show* host Stephen Colbert went on a rehearsed rant directed at Trump, in which the element of self-parody vanished at a point somewhere before this sentence: "The only thing your mouth is good for is being Vladimir Putin's cock holster." The stand-up comedian Kathy Griffin posed with a bloody severed head in the likeness of Trump. Until June 18 the Public Theater in New York was performing a version of *Julius Caesar* in which Caesar was made to look and gesticulate like Trump. Of course it trashed the play, since you render the hesitation of Brutus unintelligible if Caesar becomes the odious Trump-monster instead of the dim, weak, vain, and vaguely blustering man a little past his prime that the text portrays. Obsession with Trump has become an excuse for almost any vulgarity. Also for testing the third rail of fame in the cause of experimental valor and affected rebellion: Johnny Depp, introducing his film *The Libertine* at Glastonbury Festival, asked the audience: "When was the last time an actor assassinated a president?" We are already used to seeing these provocations followed a day or two later by an apology as insincere as it is ineffectual.

The best recourse of sanity to those who would rather defeat Trump than disgust his supporters may be simply to recall that he has at his back the massed weight and momentum of the Republican Party. It doesn't much matter who is making use of whom: they are not about to part company, while the Democrats have to defend the shrinking redoubt of just eighteen of fifty statehouses and a respectable but thoroughly confused minority in Congress. It is Republicans today who see themselves as makers of a revolution. The recent Democratic presidents, at some cost to the character of the party, espoused an ethic of moderation and trimming compromise. Doubtless the same predisposition played a large part in Obama's decision to suppress what he knew of Russian interference before the 2016 election. Presumptive stability was a good thing in itself: why roil people's temper with one more irritation? They need to believe that the system works—that was how he scored it. The assumption anyway was that Hillary would win; and fear of a rigged election was Trump's issue.

Nothing now would better serve the maturity and the invigoration of the Democrats than to give up any hope of sound advice or renewal from Bill or Hillary Clinton or Barack Obama. They were pleasant to think about, but their politics have turned out wrong, and there's nothing they can do for us now. Democrats have lost all four special elections since November; if Trump ran again tomorrow, there is a strong probability he would win. Michael Moore tweeted on June 21, after the loss by Jon Ossoff, the latest Democratic hope, to a Republican opponent in Georgia: "DNC & DCCC [Democratic National Committee and Democratic Congressional Campaign Committee] has NO idea how 2 win cause they have no message, no plan, no leaders." An exclusive concern with the Russia connection may suggest that Trump is faltering now and shaken, but on June 26 the Supreme Court temporarily upheld his revised "Muslim ban," a ninety-day suspension of travel from six Arab countries, along with a 120-day ban on all refugees, except in cases where the applicant has a bona fide relationship to someone in the United States. The anti-Trump left and center may hope for vindication when the court hears the case argued in autumn, but this in truth is a tactical victory for Trump: by the time it comes up again, the designated time of suspension may have passed; and the ban was only meant to stay in force while the government carries out a reappraisal of its vetting process. You may curse Putin and Comey and misogyny and Wisconsin, but Trump is marching through the departments and agencies with budget cuts and policy changes that will be felt for years to come. Trump is the name of a cause and not just a person, and you can only fight him with another cause. The name of it might be climate change.

5

American Breakdown

August 2018

A seasonal report on the Trump presidency had better begin
with a disclaimer. Anything one says is sure to be displaced
by some entirely unexpected thing the president does
between writing and publication. This has happened once
already, with the Putin-Trump press briefing in Helsinki
and the strange spectacle it afforded: the almost physical
manifestation of Trump's deference to Putin. It may happen
again, whether as a result of the volume of saber-rattling or
the onset of war with Iran; a decision to sack Robert
Mueller, the special counsel who is investigating meddling
in the 2016 election; a shutdown of the federal government
to extort funds for the wall with Mexico; a sudden intensi-
fication of the president's attacks on his political enemies
and accusers in pending court cases.

These eruptions of breaking news are not only possible
but certain to occur, because Trump comports himself not

as a president or even a politician, but as a reality TV host. He is a showman above all. In a process where the media are cast as reviewers, and voters as spectators, the show is getting bad reviews but doing nicely: the clear sign of success is that nobody can stop talking about the star. He keeps up the suspense with teasers and decoys and unscheduled interruptions, with changes in the sponsors and the supporting cast and production team. The way to match the Trump pace is by tweeting; but that is to play his game—a gambit the White House press corps have found irresistible. Much of the damage to US politics over the last two years has been done by the anti-Trump media themselves, with their mood of perpetual panic and their lack of imagination. But the uncanny gift of Trump is an infectious vulgarity, and with it comes the power to make his enemies act with nearly as little self-restraint as he does. The proof is in the tweets. Meanwhile his administration is well along—and not very closely watched—on its slow march through the institutions. One example can stand for many.

The US Environmental Protection Agency, created in 1970 by Richard Nixon, has been responsible—under both Democratic and Republican leadership—for a large share of the improvements we now take for granted in the restriction of toxic chemical release, fuel economy, and the safety of drinking water. Trump's first choice as administrator of the EPA, Scott Pruitt, soon after taking command, purged its website entry on climate change. (More than a year later, if you go to epa.gov/climatechange you are told the page is still being "being updated" to "reflect EPA's priorities under the leadership of President Trump and Administrator Pruitt.") Then Pruitt found a method for reducing the number of scientists on the EPA's two advisory boards. Science research lives or dies by the government grant, but under Pruitt no member of an EPA board can receive a grant. His administration weakened rules on coal ash, smog, and mercury, and cut back enforcement on toxic chemicals. "Pruitt has driven away hundreds of experienced EPA staffers and scientists," Rebecca Leber reported in the March–April issue of *Mother Jones*, "while putting old friends and industry reps in charge of key environmental decisions." The military and charter flights he booked for himself, his $2 million security detail, his payment of $120,000 to an opposition research outfit to spy on hostile journalists: a long string of such offenses tagged Pruitt as a bottom feeder, even by the grouper-and-bristleworm standard of the Trump government. In the face of complaints by scientists as well as lawmakers and journalists (including some on the far right), Trump continued to express unqualified admiration for Pruitt's performance, until the boom was lowered on July 5. A tweet announced that the president had accepted Pruitt's resignation. His replacement, Andrew Wheeler, is a former coal lobbyist who can be trusted to keep a lower profile; he has slowed the pace of Pruitt's anti-regulatory innovations, and in some cases sent a program back for reassessment. In the reign of Trump, this is what we are learning to call progress; but the truth is that climate change presents a developing catastrophe of such proportions that even the Democratic opposition has been immobilized.

A more immediate threat to the United States and the world, namely war with Iran, has been covered just as sparingly. The war may take the form of a full-scale cyber attack, with the promise of regime change; and we have not begun to imagine the possible effects. But the Democrats have expressed no more interest in Iran than they do in the six wars the US is still conducting in the Greater Middle East (Afghanistan, Iraq, Syria, Yemen, Libya, Somalia). Russia remains the obsessional concern. Not wanting to restart the Cold War might seem one of the few good ideas attributable to Trump, no matter how he came by it, but the pride of the Democrats is invested in pushing him toward renewed conflict: stiffer sanctions, cyber implants, enhanced deployments, and joint military exercises with NATO—nothing (it is said) should be "off the table." American commentators lack even a minimal awareness of the circumstances of the eastward push of NATO after 1990. President George H. W. Bush, in return for a united Germany, had promised that NATO would expand "not one inch eastward"; and the evacuation of this pledge in the years that followed, under Clinton, the younger Bush, and Obama, has rightly been considered a betrayal by Russian leaders as diverse as Gorbachev and Putin.

Putin is one of many strongmen who thrive in the East and West today—entirely comparable to Orbán, Erdoğan, and Netanyahu, and worse than the others in proportion as his power submits to fewer checks. No doubt Trump in his irregular way aspires to become a member of this company. But the geopolitical common sense of Putin's comment on Ukraine and Crimea—"I do not want to be welcomed in Sevastopol by NATO sailors"—is almost inscrutable to the unipolar press that in 2003 overwhelmingly endorsed the Iraq war. From the *New York Times* and the *New Yorker* to CNN and MSNBC, nothing has changed in the mentality of the people who arrived at that verdict fifteen years ago; and the next Democratic president, if there is one, will be under pressure to mount continuous threats against a nuclear power the Democrats have gone back to calling an adversary.

To anyone who remembers the Cold War (1947–1989), the reversal of roles is astonishing. Throughout the earlier period, it was Republicans who embraced the idea of open conflict with Russia, and Democrats who acquiesced in the arms race but tried to calm things down. A fair analogy may come from the 1850s, when the party of Jefferson and Jackson embraced slavery as their vote-getter, while the new Republicans, descendants of the Federalist Party of Adams and Washington, took their stand on anti-slavery and free labor. "I remember once being much amused," Lincoln wrote in a letter of 1859,

> at seeing two partially intoxicated men engage in a fight with their great-coats on, which fight, after a long, and rather harmless contest, ended in each having fought himself *out* of his own coat, and *into* that of the other. If the two leading parties of this day are really identical with the two in the days of Jefferson and Adams, they have performed about the same feat as the two drunken men.

In the early 1950s, the demagogue-brawler Senator Joe McCarthy pronounced the doom of New Deal bureaucrats and lawmakers to requite "twenty years of treason." Today, Congressman Adam Schiff of California—a quiet, lucid, methodical prosecutor in command of a flawless monotone—prophesies the destruction of American democracy at the hands of Putin.

As in the 1850s, the change of clothes has gone both ways. Here is Patrick Buchanan, a speechwriter for Nixon and Reagan, wondering at the double standard of the anti-Russian Democrats: "Many Putin actions we condemn were reactions to what we did. Russia annexed Crimea bloodlessly. But did not the US bomb Serbia for 78 days to force Belgrade to surrender her cradle province of Kosovo? How was that more moral than what Putin did in Crimea?" No writer for the liberal press in 2018 would have ventured to ask these questions.

Left-wing Democrats commonly refer to Trump as a fascist. But there is no fascist militia to complete the picture, and the wildest accusations have been made against Trump with an impunity unknown to the resisters of Mussolini and Hitler. The lower courts, too, are standing up against this president with a fair degree of independence, especially in cases related to immigration. Yet in two respects, the authoritarian danger does resemble that of the 1930s in Europe. Trump believes that a unitary bond links him to the real people. He is their voice. And Republican moderates have almost extinguished themselves as a political species. Though party grandees as various as McCain, Romney, G. W. and Jeb Bush declined to support Trump against Clinton in 2016, and the Tea Party favorite Ted Cruz postponed his endorsement until the eleventh hour, congressional Republicans have settled on a policy of cooperation for the sake of party political advantage. Should one apply the word "collaborator" to such people? The word has a certain appropriateness, in spite of the incompleteness of the analogy. The Republican Party began by legitimating Trump and has gone on to normalize the extreme aberration in a way that recalls the passive compliance of King Victor Emmanuel III in 1922 and Field Marshal Hindenburg in 1933.

Yet it is the "resistance" warriors in the popular culture who have gone furthest to take political confrontation to a perilous edge. Robert De Niro led a cheer of "Fuck Trump" at the Tony Awards, and received a standing ovation. In a comic monologue, Samantha Bee buttonholed Ivanka Trump: "You know, Ivanka, that's a beautiful photo of you and your child, but let me just say, one mother to another: Do something about your dad's immigration practices, you feckless cunt!" With the enforcement of Trump's zero-tolerance policy against illegal immigrants, the enraged of the left have continued to up the ante. Judd Apatow: "Trump is a Nazi. The debate is over." Peter Fonda: "We should rip Barron Trump from his mother's arms and put him in a cage with pedophiles." Advisers to the president and members of his cabinet have been mobbed and jeered, denied service in restaurants, and harassed at home; and more such actions have been urged by the woke contingent of the Democratic Party. Representative Maxine Waters advised protesters to "create a crowd" and physically "push back on" associates of Trump. Manners aside, the trouble with such tactics is that they serve to justify an equal and opposite reaction. To the ordinary non-political sensibility, they also prompt reflexive pity for the victims, and squander whatever moral advantage the opposition may have gained from the lowness and brutality of Trump himself. Police, for the most part, haven't yet shown a pro-Trump disposition, and Democrats should want to keep things that way. Among officers of law enforcement at all levels, Trump's role as an instigator of popular disorders is the strongest point against him.

Democrats have reason to style themselves as a party of order, which also must mean obedience to laws, since they are depending on the courts and the intelligence community to save the country from Trump—depending on them, indeed, with a simple fervor that approaches the condition of prayer. And yet for some time, going back as far as the summer of 2016, there has been a civil war inside the FBI. It can be traced to a division of judgment regarding the gravity of Hillary Clinton's offense in using a private and insecure email server for State Department business that included classified documents. The consensus was that her conduct had been careless and wrong, but that it by no means warranted prosecution for giving aid and comfort to enemies of the United States. A faction in the New York field office of the bureau disagreed; and, using their connections with the ex-mayor of New York Rudolph Giuliani, they orchestrated a series of selective leaks to throw doubt on the decision by James Comey as director of the FBI to close the investigation. The last and most effective of their leaks concerned the late discovery of a laptop that might contain emails to inculpate Clinton after all. This forced the hand of Comey and prompted his announcement in late October 2016 that the case was being reopened.

What has become clear only lately, with the release of the Justice Department inspector-general's report, is that Comey acted then—as he had done a few months earlier in announcing that Clinton would not be prosecuted—in the belief that the election would certainly be won by Clinton. The all-important thing was to preserve a common trust in the stability and impartiality of the legal institutions then being undermined by the Trump campaign. Hence the reopening of the investigation in October. Hence, too, the decision by the attorney general, Loretta Lynch, to let Comey make the original announcement, critical of Clinton, which ended the investigation in July. Lynch had compromised her appearance of impartiality by a long and unexplained private conversation with Bill Clinton; and she, like Comey, wanted the institutions of justice to have shown themselves fair in the aftermath of Trump's defeat. Only the election didn't come out as expected. From causes that long predate the election, Comey and Mueller in any case regard Trump as a criminal who was never caught; and Trump knows it. The disposition of all these actors makes the conduct of the Justice Department, the FBI, the special counsel, and the courts the central drama in the United States today.

How does he get away with it? Trump speaks as one of the certified rich who understands the feelings of those lower down the ladder. He is the incarnation of the new gilded age without pretense—rich without being refined—and he knows very well that hatred of the other side is the main reason one-third of the country will follow wherever he leads. It may be doubted that the same one-third would call him a good man, but another figure is sobering: 87 percent of Republicans approve of his presidency. They hated the Hillary Clinton who called them "deplorables" and the media who said voters for Trump were "angry white men."

The job of a decent and skillful politician in a democracy is to appeal to the interests of people without feeding their prejudices. After 2008, who gave these people much to like? Not Obama, who two years after the financial collapse told them their troubles were over, except for some economic "headwinds" that would lighten up soon. Obama's $65 million book deal and $50 million Netflix deal, his photo-op vacations on Branson's island and Geffen's yacht and Tahiti, his design for tearing up the Chicago Olmsted Park to lay down the Obama Presidential Library, which will host a yoga center—these things are noticed in the right-wing press and the gutter Twittersphere. They make Obama out to be one more liberal hypocrite; whereas with Trump the almost-avowed corruption adds to the overall zest of the presentation.

People often speak of Trump's flouting of norms as a trait no less hostile to constitutional democracy than his probable outlawry. It can seem an elusive observation because it points to a new fact. His capricious use of authority is as maddening as his brutality of address. He can initiate a policy and then countermand it under pressure, as he did in mid-June against his own atrocious order to separate children from their illegal immigrant parents. But then on a third day, he will announce that none of this is any good: the families should just be "sent back." Tweets are his instrument, irritant, and weapon of choice. In the small hours, he can send up a flare of self-praise, throw down a libelous challenge to a reporter, and insult one of his detractors in show business or in the Democratic leadership; and all of it will be news. Twitter has also become the medium by which his most determined opponents regularly transmit their reactions—the standard format now for a public statement without a call to reporters—and it has made Trump the dominant American politician without a shadow of rivalry. If the next presidential election were held today, he would be the Republican nominee and he would probably win. A Gallup poll on June 18 showed him at 45 percent approval; this dropped a notch or two after the Helsinki debacle; but Rasmussen (a more accurate predictor of the 2016 election) now has him at 50 percent. The figures are comparable to Obama's in 2012.

The only Democratic leaders who are known to many Americans are Joe Biden, Bernie Sanders, and Elizabeth Warren, and their combined age is 220. How did that happen? The Clinton-Obama dollar tree cast a shade for a quarter-century in which smaller political fortunes have struggled even to breathe. Meanwhile, the Democrats remain in denial about the charm of Trump, the force of his personality for a certain crowd. He has an effective voice, and by many accounts can show a flattering attentiveness to other people's need of attention; his manner, when things are going well, is self-depreciating in a likeable way. Consider a characteristic move: he recently tore away the first page of a speech and let it float to the ground; a written speech is so boring, he said. A stunt, but the crowd loved it. He can slip a head-on challenge as well as the most seasoned of clowns; in a tight spot, he has the ingenuity of a weasel. The moral and political nastiness that Trump calls up with such ease is laced with high spirits.

If he outlasts the Mueller inquiry and runs for a second term, what will it take to beat him? Trump never explains anything. He doesn't have the sort of mind that could construct an explanation, but he spits out slogans and names, and he won the Republican nomination partly through the vulgar wit of certain nicknames: Low Energy Jeb, for example. He is a scattershot cartoonist and some of it sticks. Two weapons are indispensable if you want to run against someone like that. You must be a good, simple, and memorable explainer; and you must have the humor and presence of mind to parry the insults he deals out fast and loose. There is plenty of talent in the Democratic field, but nobody yet with those talents well developed.

All of his confidence and shameless exuberance were on display in a back-from-Singapore talk on June 15 to assorted members of the White House press corps. He began by referring to General Flynn, his first national security adviser. A major suspicion about Trump's early months in office turns on the eighteen days that elapsed between a warning by the acting attorney general—Flynn had lied about his contact with Russians, and could be compromised—and Trump's eventual decision to sack him. Flynn has since pleaded guilty to lying to the FBI and is cooperating with the Mueller inquiry, but the president hopes he won't cooperate too much; and this was the context for a characteristic improvisation:

> I feel badly for General Flynn. He's lost his house, he's lost his life. And some people say he lied and some people say he didn't lie. I mean really it turned out maybe he didn't lie. How can you do that because who's lied more than Comey? Comey lied a tremendous amount.

Here, the exaggeration about Flynn—"He's lost his life"—is ambiguous between the loss of a career and physical death. You are made to feel that Flynn, anyway, was owed a deeper compassion than the press and lawmen allowed. Then Trump slots in the shrug and the jam-up: some people say this, some say that—who can know?—opening a path for the two-pronged slither of "really" and "it turned out." These words are logically vacuous placeholders, but for Trump's audience they have the force of material facts. "Maybe" and "really" and "turned out" must mean that Flynn *didn't* lie. And the finishing touch: Comey! Suddenly the despised former head of the FBI is hauled back on stage and all other considerations vanish. We may hardly notice that the fact isn't a fact; no one ever accused Comey of lying. The charge is that he took too much authority to himself, usurped the proper duties of the attorney general when he chose to give the press briefing on Hillary Clinton's emails himself, and inserted ad lib criticisms of her conduct in what should have been a strictly legal report. The only "lie" Trump had in his head was Comey's assurance that he, Trump, wasn't personally under investigation. On other evidence, Trump came to believe he was a target, and he fired Comey accordingly.

A reporter at the same briefing asked about a coming congressional vote on two immigration bills—the one spelling out zero tolerance for illegal cases and the other a more moderate bill. "Would you sign either one of those?" Trump replied, without missing a beat: "I'm looking at both of them. I certainly wouldn't sign the more moderate one. I need a bill that gives this country tremendous border security. I have to have that. We have to get rid of catch-and-release. We have to have the wall. If we don't have the wall, there is no bill." He hadn't a clue what was in either bill, but what the hell—wall, bill—the words are almost as close as Iraq and Iran, and Trump's answer was a napkin waved to conceal a disappearing rabbit. His reflex is dependable and the thought-balloon must have said: "To me, I'm looking at them both, and moderate sounds bad, tremendous is good, we need something tremendous, and the border wall, really maybe it turns out it's all about the wall." The wall with Mexico stands for every material change he can effect by sheer incantation.

Trump can now claim three achievements, two of them widely popular in spite of media disapproval and the third so predictable as to make no new enemies. There is the Republican tax cut, which benefits the very rich but offers a temporary boost for small businesses, too—and unemployment in May fell to 3.9 percent, its lowest level since 2000. There is the promise of denuclearization of the Korean peninsula, its first steps signaled by the return of hostages, the United States and allies' refraining from joint military exercises, and the North Korean destruction of test facilities. The process has only just begun, but the foreign policy establishment, from the Council on Foreign Relations to Fareed Zakaria, have struck an odd posture by declaring peaceful relations with North Korea to be impossible and undesirable. The president of South Korea appears to think otherwise, and his view should count for something. Trump's third success he did little directly to promote and a good deal to frustrate: on June 26, the Supreme Court ended his battle against lower court decisions by approving his travel ban (twice revised) on the countries he has designated hotbeds of terrorism. The final version added North Korea and Venezuela to the banned countries of the Greater Middle East, to give the thing a nondenominational complexion. The real cruelty of the man came through in the first version, which stopped travelers with legitimate visas. The cruelty has emerged, more shockingly, in the "deterrence" policy of child separation at the Mexican border. In answer to both actions, protests were mounted with a punctual energy and a force of numbers that caused Trump to reverse field.

Almost never mentioned in these debates is the fact that the United States bears considerable responsibility for the influx at its southern border. Among the countries supplying the heaviest count of refugees are Guatemala, Honduras, and El Salvador, each of them a site of US military intervention or subversion that fomented civil violence, the most recent instance being the military coup in Honduras in early 2009 (supported by Obama's State Department under Hillary Clinton). Should the Democrats be silent about the long past of the troubles at the border? By putting a minus sign in front of every Trump policy, they have anyway spared themselves the work of arriving at reasonable positions of their own. Consider ICE, the federal authority for Immigration and Customs Enforcement. This began as a post-2001 innovation of Cheney and Bush, its powers were then expanded under Obama, and people who know its oppressive tactics are cheering the slogan "Abolish ICE." Good, but what will you put in its place? A 1996 federal law permits the deportation of legal noncitizen residents who have committed violent crimes. Would the Democrats repeal that law?

Again, the party that passed Obama's Iran nuclear deal has seemed indifferent to the preparations for war with Iran that became impossible to mistake when Trump pulled out of the agreement. The chance of war grew steeper when Trump appointed as his second secretary of state Mike Pompeo, a militarist with a particular hatred for Iran, and as his third national security adviser John Bolton, an anti-Muslim fanatic of the Cheney circle. Leaders of both parties continue to nurse the most dangerous illusions about the prospect of regime change in Iran, with the People's Mujahedin of Iran and other sympathetic terrorist outfits presumably counted on to assist. What seems to be contemplated is an attack by the triple alliance of the Saudis, the United Arab Emirates, and Israel, with the United States in the background.

This brings up an awkward question about a country that has meddled in US elections far more persistently and with larger measurable effects than Russia: namely, Israel. The most important financial backer of Netanyahu is also the most important backer of Trump, the casino billionaire Sheldon Adelson, who gave $83 million to Republican candidates in 2016 and will do more in 2020, provided the move of the US embassy to Jerusalem is followed by the war Netanyahu wants. The Netanyahu-Adelson-Trump connection is well known to the US and Israeli press, but it has been emphasized by only a few journalists, including Peter Stone, Amy Wilentz, and Philip Weiss. Whatever the malignity of Putin's design, he will never equal the success of Netanyahu's speeches to Congress in 2011 and 2015, which received a combined total of fifty-five standing ovations.

Yet any American half-persuaded to try and think about something other than Russia was dragged all the way back by the startling performance of Trump in Helsinki. He was polite and deferential and, though a good deal taller than Putin, he looked to be the less confident man: it took something from his size. He can still refer to the sanctions he is enforcing, and his effort to take Russian gas away from Europe. Yet his reply to a blunt question about Russian meddling—"President Putin, he just said it's not Russia. I will say this, I don't see any reason why it would be . . . I will tell you that President Putin was extremely strong and powerful in his denial"—left American politicians and commentators spinning for days afterward. Trump tried to walk it back by saying he had meant to say "I don't see why it *wouldn't* be" but got tangled in the confusion of double negatives. And it's true that normally his thinking would be able to accommodate both senses: why *would* they—because you keep on saying I needed them to win the election, but I didn't need them, why would I need them? On the other hand, face it, the Russians spy on us and try to interfere, and we do it to them, so, yeah, why wouldn't they? (A scholar at Carnegie Mellon University, Dov Levin, recently calculated that between 1946 and 2000, the United States intervened in eighty-one foreign elections, while Russia did it in thirty-six.) The only trouble was, the "wouldn't" could not possibly fit the sequence here. Putin truly assured him and, having accepted the assurance that they didn't do it, Trump sees no reason why they would have or why he should doubt Putin's word against that of his intelligence services. About the entire performance, it was hard to believe Trump could have acted as he did unless Putin had some sort of hold over him. It was almost as hard to believe that a guilty man would lower his defenses so artlessly.

Helsinki has proved to be only the latest of the last straws that for Trump are never the end. It seems to have had an effect as fleeting as the *Access Hollywood* tape—where he spoke of the celebrity prerogative of grabbing women by their private parts—which the Democrats thought would cause the collapse of his campaign in October 2016. Midterm elections generally revolve around domestic policy in any case, and November 2018 will have at least one domestic subject in full view: Trump's nomination of the conservative judge Brett Kavanaugh to fill the vacant seat on the Supreme Court. Democrats reacted to the nomination with outrage almost exclusively concerned with a possible court reversal on abortion. Hardly a word was said about surveillance, state secrecy, and executive power, issues on which Kavanaugh holds views compatible with the presidency of George W. Bush. But this was a conventional choice, by Trump standards, and Democrats up for re-election in moderate or Republican states will find Kavanaugh hard to vote against.

The Democratic Party has encountered another recent perplexity—a fresh and visible left wing it doesn't know what to do with. One symptom of the party's incapacity was the House Democratic leader Nancy Pelosi's dismissive response to the New York primary victory of Alexandria Ocasio-Cortez: a young politician, resourceful at organizing and irrepressibly energetic, who describes herself as a democratic socialist. Her triumph brought irrelevant comparisons to Obama; Ocasio-Cortez is, in fact, a left activist, as Obama never was. She has already been out campaigning for Democratic House candidates in Michigan and Kansas. A party with a working brain would respond to this stroke of good fortune by thinking hard about how to explain democracy and socialism to voters outside New York City.

Comey's memoir has now surpassed the combined sales of Michael Wolff's portrait of the Trump White House, *Fire and Fury*, and Hillary Clinton's election elegy *What Happened*. The book, written in an idiom identical to the one he uses in interviews and press briefings, is clearly the work of an un-ghosted author, and it contains passages most unusual for an official memoir:

> There is a place I have visited on the coast of North Carolina where two barrier islands come close together. In the narrow passageway between them, the waters of the Atlantic Ocean meet the waters of the huge and shallow sound that lies behind the islands. There is turbulence in that place and waves appear to break even though no land is visible. I imagine that the leaders of the Department of Justice stand at that spot, between the turbulent waters of the political world and the placid waters of the apolitical sound. Their job is to respond to the political imperatives of the president and the voters who elected him, while also protecting the apolitical work of the thousands of agents, prosecutors, and staff who make up the bulk of the institution. So long as the leaders understand the turbulence, they can find their footing. If they stumble, the ocean water overruns the

sound and the department has become just another political organ. Its independent role in American life has been lost and the guardians of justice have drowned.

This depth of formal piety cannot be faked; the passage shows the burden (as Comey sees it) of maintaining constitutional and legal restraints on Donald Trump.

All the loose talk of the mainstream media about Mueller and Russia may have hidden the gravity of the contest between Trump and legality. And it is by no means certain that legality will win. The larger question is therefore whether law-abidingness will remain the pattern of American society. No doubt, the election of Trump was the efficient cause of the crisis, but it is worth considering the likely state of the nation had Hillary Clinton won. Depending on the appetite for mayhem that Trump himself chose to unleash, the country might easily have become as ungovernable as it is today; and that prospect was in Comey's mind when he wrote about the necessity of keeping one's footing in the turbulence.

A whole new set of actors have entered the scene, as they do every few months in the Trump presidency. Rudy Giuliani, the voice of the anti-Clinton faction of the FBI, is now the chief lawyer for Trump; and in an early pronouncement in that role, he declared that Trump has the power to pardon himself. The idea is absurd, yet no more so than many others that people have nodded at: for example, the reiterated assurance that Mexico will pay for the wall. Giuliani has avowed that his strategy is to wear down the popular trust of Mueller, so that an assertion by Mueller will be no more credible than a denial by Trump.

The invention of the liberal state originally derived from the need for balance in the parts of government; the presence, as Locke put it, of an "umpire" and the absence of any power capable of acting as the judge in its own cause. Yet for half a century now, there have been signs of a growing non-attachment to the rule of law at the heights of American politics. The Nixon pardon was only the clearest example. Think of the Iran-Contra pardons; Bill Clinton's pardon of the most exorbitant tax defrauder in American history, Marc Rich (also a donor to the Clinton Presidential Library); or Obama's refusal to prosecute anyone implicated in the financial collapse of 2007–2008 or the torture regime of Guantánamo and Abu Ghraib. Nixon befouled the 1968 election in a manner Putin could only have dreamed of—the facts are now established—by having Anna Chennault tell the leaders of South Vietnam not to negotiate. The Reagan campaign team appears to have done much the same in 1980 by bargaining to have the return of American hostages from Iran delayed until after the election: their release added a pleasant grace note to his inauguration day. Trump, it must be said, worked faster than his predecessors when he issued early pardons to Lewis Libby (convicted of lying to the FBI to conceal his outing of a CIA agent) and Dinesh D'Souza (convicted of illegal campaign contributions and false statements to the Federal Election Commission).

Criminality at the highest levels has been overlooked, redefined, extenuated, and forgiven. Trump's acts of a similar nature were thus condoned by anticipation, and a long train of bogus reversals has eased the way for his implied offer of pardons in the Russia scandal. Democrats are right to be haunted by the indications that in 2016 it happened again, but they are wrong to suppose there can be just one cause: that Trump stole the election by getting Russia to corrupt the system. They neglect the possibility that he is implicated in a general corruption by the variety and extent of his connections with people who did the work. Further back, from arrangements made twenty years ago and more, it stands to reason that Trump is deeply in debt to Russian oligarchs. He was in real estate, he always needed loans, he had become a pariah on Wall Street; and if you need big money in real estate and can't get it at home and want to have it laundered, whom do you go to? Whether all this can be linked to the 2016 election is another story. Even as the facts grow harder to dodge—with even Trump saying, in early August, that Donald Jr. met Russians in Trump Tower to get dirt on Hillary—Republicans are unlikely to make obstruction of justice an impeachment charge. Driven equally by cynicism and cowardice, they will continue on the collaboration path.

The trial in Virginia of Paul Manafort, Trump's former campaign manager, is proceeding at a fast pace; and before the end of the year, Mueller is expected to conclude his indictments and submit his findings to the Justice Department. Almost a dozen advisers, helpers, cronies, and fixers have been investigated—Manafort, Stone, Cohen, Papadopoulos, Kushner, Trump Jr., Page, and Flynn, among others—but Trump may have given them a free hand with Russia while keeping himself plausibly in the dark. We now know that Manafort made $60 million working for the pro-Russian President Yanukovych in Ukraine. So the weights in the scale against Trump are heavy and getting heavier; he can feel the exposure coming. And the relationship of the lawmen to the president is as transparent as it is intricate: they know he knows they know. But defeating this presidency and preserving the rule of law are not two elements of a single undertaking. The tasks are distinct, and success in the first venture will depend on persistence in the second.

6

Midterm Fever

March 2019

Between October and January, the ground seemed to be rolling underfoot, but the tremors have died down. The two weeks before the November election saw the collapse of Donald Trump's midterm strategy, which had consisted almost entirely of an effort to foment immigration panic. After he lost his Republican congressional majority on November 6, he made a feint at appeasing the Democrats, with a deal to keep government running, then a threat to invoke emergency powers to build the wall his right-wing base demands, and at last a hint of moderate conciliation. Behind the shifts and starts, the actually existing Trump administration was falling apart in several directions. It was also adding new members who commit it to policies that will invert the whole tendency of Trump in 2016. The new secretary of state, Mike Pompeo, and the national security adviser, John Bolton, are advocates of US force projection whose appetite for wars can only frustrate Trump's announced purpose to withdraw from the wars we are already in. The extent to which this president understands so simple a fact about a government he nominally leads is hard to gauge. But in the Trump presidency so far, the moments of extreme hazard have gone as fast as they came. The underlying condition is chaos, renewable by whim, chance, or microscopic provocation.

Trump hired Bolton and Pompeo at least partly because they share his passionate hostility toward Iran. It didn't occur to him that they would be lukewarm supporters of his agreement with North Korea and do their best to thwart his pledge to detach US armed forces from Afghanistan and Syria. In one of the morning hours he could spare from the wall with Mexico, a thought of Iran returned to the mind of Trump, and on January 30 he published a tweet denouncing the Senate testimony of his intelligence chiefs Dan Coats, Gina Haspel, and Christopher Wray: they were "naïve" for concluding that Iran wasn't working on a nuclear weapon. Half of Trump's argument for getting the US out of the P5+1 agreement had been that the nuclear danger was real. (The other half was the description of Iran as "the world's leading sponsor of terror"—a misleading Israeli contribution to American political discourse.) To be told there was nothing to the WMD argument clearly disappointed Trump as much as the 2007 National Intelligence Estimate had disappointed Bush and Cheney when it arrived at the same conclusion. They had planned a full propaganda blitz followed by another war—a war that Bolton and Pompeo still have on the drawing board—but to justify it now, Trump's neoconservative add-ons will have to hire a new intelligence community.

Ever since the hostage crisis of 1979–81, the very idea of Iran has triggered in millions of Americans a sensation of dread, based on no knowledge whatsoever. To recall a superstitious fear as drastic and persistent, you have to go back to the idea of Injun Country in the old West. But Bolton and Pompeo are men of large ambitions: even as they were reviving the memory of a familiar enemy in the Persian Gulf, they turned the popular discontents of Venezuela into an international crisis by recognizing the opposition leader, Juan Guaidó, as the legitimate president. Pompeo went further when he imposed new sanctions and told the world that every country must now "pick a side." Like many such messages from US leaders, the words emanated from that rhetorical limbo where a moral precept has the air of a command and vice versa. (Barack Obama: "The only way that the Syrian civil war will end . . . is . . . a government without Bashar Assad"; George W. Bush: "Either you are with us or you are with the terrorists.") To judge by their previous careers, neither Bolton nor Pompeo shares Trump's conceit that he can destroy the Iranian regime by a method short of war; on the other hand, Trump may actually be tempted by the promise of military action south of the border, where the US can show its muscle quickly and with impunity.

With these new advisers, Trump is more effectively cornered than he may have realized when he appointed them. Both are inside players with sharp elbows. They have named Elliott Abrams as special envoy to Venezuela—a sign of the warrior diplomacy they are also building up with second-echelon choices at state and the National Security Council. This is the same Elliott Abrams who organized the Reagan State Department's support for the governments of El Salvador and Guatemala when they committed atrocities with US backing, the same Abrams who brokered the shipment of arms to the Nicaraguan Contras for their attacks on "soft targets" (that is, civilians). On February 1, Pompeo clinched his demonstration that the Bush–Cheney doctrine was back by declaring US withdrawal from the Intermediate-Range Nuclear Forces Treaty: an action Trump had been warned against by Mikhail Gorbachev as well as Vladimir Putin. At a point like this, the standup comic says, *But seriously, folks.* The fatal gift of Trump is to inspire a sort of laughter that disarms contempt by complicity.

Throughout the last four months, in the president's daily tweets and in the mainstream media, the prospect of attacking a nation of 80 million or starving a nation of 30 million was a blip on the screen beside the "ongoing national conversation" about the border wall. Trump pulled off the wildest stunt of his first two years when, in late October, he dispatched to the border 5,200 active-duty troops, on the pretext that the army alone could defend US citizens from the caravan of refugees heading north—many of them violent, some of them terrorists, according to Trump. The distraction might have gone some way to blunt his losses in the midterm election, but for two surprising events that nothing could steer to his advantage. In the last week of October, thirteen package bombs were sent in the mail to Barack Obama, Hillary Clinton, Joe Biden, George Soros,

CNN, and other political and media opponents of Trump. None of them exploded, but the suspect captured on October 26 turned out to be a Trump supporter, with telltale stickers and slogans plastered over the van he lived in. The following day, eleven Jews were murdered at the Tree of Life synagogue in Pittsburgh. The man charged with the crime was an anti-Semite who despised Trump as a weakling incapable of defending white America. Neither the attempted terror bombings nor the mass shooting could be linked to the president, but these events were impossible to dissociate from the brutality of Trump's words and gestures, the mayhem he is a sponsor of, the things and people he makes unhinged. The bombs and the mass murder took the border out of the news, and the Democrats picked up forty seats in Congress—the upper end of their most optimistic hopes. In the House they now command a majority of 235–199.

Midterm congressional defeats of a sitting president are a common stimulus for reshuffling the cabinet. The Republican losses in 2006 prompted the younger Bush to drop Donald Rumsfeld as secretary of defense and accelerated his loss of confidence in Dick Cheney. But as usual with Trump, the scale of the thing dwarfs every preceding instance. On December 20 the secretary of defense, James Mattis, resigned after Trump tweeted his vow of withdrawal from Syria. This led to a reiteration, by policy experts along with many Democrats and almost all the mainstream media, of the moral importance of staying in Syria. Solemn admonitions were combined with praise of Mattis as the adult in the room, but no one stopped to ask why Mattis had jibbed at this exercise of the president's power as commander-in-chief while saying nothing against the abuse of the army in a counterfeit emergency on the border with Mexico. By the time he resigned, in any case, a house-cleaning of the periodic Trumpian sort was underway. The attorney general, Jeff Sessions, was sacked on November 7, the day after the midterm election; Trump's chief of staff, John Kelly, was dismissed on December 8; and the secretary of the interior, Ryan Zinke, resigned under suspicion of corruption on December 15. So at the start of the new year, the administration had an acting secretary of the interior, an acting secretary of defense (a Boeing executive Trump likes for his corporate know-how), and an acting attorney general (a freelance lawyer who drew Trump's attention defending him on Fox TV). A new chief of staff was brought in to replace Kelly in a job description which the known character of Trump makes nonsense of.

Such unnerving changes of personnel—often punctuated by a fanfare of derision or mockery in presidential tweets—have become a characteristic feature of the Trump White House, an arrhythmia which renders all estimates uncertain. Another aspect of the disorder, by now almost as familiar, is the passage of Trump's loyalists and former campaign officials from scandal to indictment and from indictment to trial and prison. Paul Manafort, the second manager of the 2015–16 presidential campaign, was convicted in August on eight of eighteen counts in a Virginia federal court, and faces a longer sentence for having breached his plea agreement by lying to investigators. In December, Maria Butina, a Russian who had entered the US on a student visa, pleaded guilty to the charge of conspiracy to act as an illegal foreign agent; she had successfully contacted elements of the Republican Party, the National Prayer Breakfast, and the National Rifle Association. Even if, as James Bamford has argued, Butina was a freelance gun enthusiast and her indictment a case of fantastic overreach by the FBI, it deepened the impression of an espionage implosion in the vicinity of Trump. Michael Flynn, Trump's first national security adviser, pleaded guilty of lying to the FBI about his discussion of sanctions with the Russian ambassador Sergey Kislyak. His sentence was postponed by a DC district court in December, with a strong indication that he will serve prison time. The judge observed in passing that Flynn had betrayed his country. The purpose of the delay was to allow him to assist another, possibly related, prosecution in Virginia.

Trump's personal lawyer and fixer Michael Cohen was sentenced in December in a New York federal court for tax fraud, lying to Congress, and paying hush money to prevent Trump's affairs with two women coming to light during the campaign. It has since emerged that Trump's own negotiations for a Trump Tower Moscow continued throughout his run for president. "From the day I announced to the day I won," as he allowed his new lawyer Rudy Giuliani to reveal: a fact about which Cohen has admitted he lied to Congress. The significance of these concessions is that the time of the negotiation dovetails with the public pleas by Trump to eliminate sanctions on Russia. The inference requires very little imagination: he needed sanctions lifted to get the loans from sanctioned Russian banks in order to build his Moscow hotel. Trump has denied telling anyone to lie about anything, while admitting (in another message delivered via Giuliani): "He does remember conversations about Moscow.

He does remember the letter of intent. He does remember, after that, fleeting conversations." Cohen's prime Moscow contact was Felix Sater, an American real-estate developer with ties to organized crime, who wrote to Cohen in late 2015 that together they could "get all of Putin's team to buy in on this" so that "our boy can become president of the USA and we can engineer it." On June 14, 2016, Cohen met Sater in Trump Tower New York and said he wouldn't be traveling to Russia after all. June 14 was also the day the *Washington Post* ran the first story on the hacking of the Democratic National Committee.

There were to be further discussions by other actors— above all, the Trump Tower meeting with Russians to pick up information on Hillary Clinton, to which Don Jr. agreed with alacrity. The next turn of the screw is an arrest and a trial away: federal prosecutors may put Cohen on the stand to say how he kept both Trump and Don Jr. in the loop on the Moscow deal—a fact that would show Don Jr.'s state of mind when he accepted a meeting that offered opposition research in exchange for sanctions relief. Quite possibly, a profit to the Trump Organization of $300 million was riding on it; and to judge by Cohen's testimony thus far, he probably knows enough to invalidate Don Jr.'s claim of innocent political curiosity. Trump, reverting to gangland argot, has called Cohen "a rat" and advised his Justice Department to investigate Cohen's father-in-law; but the inquiry by the special counsel, Robert Mueller, keeps moving ahead undeterred, and on January 25 another close associate of Trump's, Roger Stone, who professed to have advance knowledge of a WikiLeaks release of DNC documents, was arrested at his home in

Fort Lauderdale. Stone is charged with seven felonies, including lying to the FBI, lying to Congress, and witness tampering. His alleged collaborators in the Trump–WikiLeaks connection, Jerome Corsi and Randy Credico, have been subpoenaed by Mueller. Some protection may be afforded Trump by his nominee as the next attorney general, William Barr, a right-wing Republican with a belief in a strong chief executive; Barr was expeditiously confirmed by the Republican Senate, and he will work to keep Trump in office; the interesting question is whether he will allow the Mueller findings to be published and, if so, with what redactions. The fear that Mueller might be summarily fired seems to have lifted. But given the possibility that Barr will filter and obscure the Mueller report, as Cheney buried CIA challenges regarding the international danger posed by Iraq, the team conducting the probe doubtless have a backup plan. Mueller's discretion up to this point has been his most valuable asset. His performance has exceeded every expectation of rigor, and the person now at the center of the persons of interest is the president of the United States.

New York bankers "always knew the Trumps were dirty," a retired banker told me. If they owed 10 percent on a collapsed enterprise, they would leave the investors holding the bag. Appropriately, the financial forensics analyst Andrew Weissmann was among the first appointments announced by Mueller. In late November, a German police raid on the Deutsche Bank offices in Frankfurt looked like another piece of the puzzle—especially if one recalled the subpoena of the bank by Mueller a year earlier. Readers of

Bob Woodward's *Fear* might also remember Trump's consternation on hearing his lawyer John Dowd speak of Mueller's interest in Deutsche Bank. Woodward reported the reaction without inquiring into its possible cause, but the moment stands out from the mood of that book—an explosion amid the general sprawl of improvisation and inconsequence.

Why could Deutsche Bank matter so much? A knowledgeable veteran of the corporate and finance world explained it as follows. When the New York real estate market and the big banks threw Trump by the roadside, he had to find other sources and shelters to rely on. Deutsche Bank was one. The many Russian purchasers of Trump apartments were another. The Russian government, as Cohen's testimony showed, was a third. An excellent investigative report by David Barstow, Susanne Craig, and Russ Buettner, in the *New York Times* on October 7, 2018, took us back to the origins of Trump's business ethic: he followed his father, Fred Trump, sailing close to the wind of outlaw behavior, and learned how to hide the evidence under one shell or another. It began with New York housing, in rental and repair scams. For example: purchase boilers for your apartments from a standard manufacturer, but run the billing through a shell company; pay the manufacturer the list price and inflate it by 20 or 25 percent on padded invoices; send the overflow to members of the Trump family. Gradually, Donald scaled his methods to encompass far more complex designs—labyrinthine patterns of chicanery that would require massive resources for a prosecutor to unwind and bring charges against. Probably that is what ended the New York investigation of the Trump Soho project. And, as an outlaw strategy for a billionaire, it was hard to beat: no state or federal agency could justify the time and money necessary to pursue him. Not, anyway, until he became president and treated the Justice Department as if it were another branch of New York real estate. It now seems likely that Mueller will produce overwhelming evidence of money laundering, as well as tax, business, and bank fraud, and the deceptive use of a charitable foundation for personal aggrandizement. Some of the evidence will tie the president to Russian and Saudi influence; the rest, handed over to the Internal Revenue Service and the State of New York, is likely to implicate officers of the Trump Organization who are also members of the Trump family.

The question remains whether the citizenry—between 30 and 40 percent of eligible voters—who register across-the-board approval of Trump will accept the ouster of a president solely on the grounds that his success was built on corruption and he won the presidency with a conflict of interest between his business and his country. The word "collusion," which has no legal status, has rooted itself in popular journalism to describe the putative cooperation between Trump and Russia, but the legal term "conspiracy" has a sharper definition and a high standard of proof. Democrats, in a way, have made things easier for Trump by harping on Putin, with the clear suggestion that a written or recorded bargain to subvert the election is waiting to be discovered. That would qualify as conspiracy. But such evidence may not exist; and by fixing the public mind on the idea of collusion, at once vague and foursquare, Democrats along with anti-Trump media like CNN and

MSNBC have blurred the difference between a dereliction of constitutional duty and a violation of criminal law. None of it will precipitate a decorous surrender by Trump. Unlike Nixon, he will deny to the end and blame it on "the witch hunt." Fox talkers like Sean Hannity and Rush Limbaugh and their common source the *Drudge Report*—whose influence the Democrats have long underrated from a mixture of snobbery, pride, and laziness—will goad the president to stand his ground. Trump will encourage his base to defend him, by whatever means they choose.

The plausibility of impeachment charges, if it comes to that, will depend on the accumulated mass of the circumstantial evidence. "The lieutenants in Trump's orbit," as Garrett Graff noted in a report for *Wired*, "rebuffed precisely zero of the known Russian overtures. In fact, quite the opposite. Each approach was met with enthusiasm, and a request for more"; all of them, from George Papadopoulos to Don Jr., "not only allegedly took every offered meeting, and returned every email or phone call, but appeared to take overt action to encourage further contact." The lies told by the Trump team, lies known to his Russian contacts, would provide a foreign power with immense leverage on the president. What, then, counts as circumstantial evidence? The earliest modern definitions come from Bentham and Burke; and in the case at hand, Burke's sketch of the idea (in a 1794 report for the House of Commons in the impeachment of Warren Hastings) is both pertinent and suggestive. Partisans of Hastings had said a great proportion of the evidence of corruption against the governor-general of Bengal was merely circumstantial. Burke pointed out that all evidence apart from confession derives from circumstances, and evidence of this sort "when it is most abundant in circumstances . . . is much superior to positive proof"; for it comprehends

> all the acts of the party,—all things that explain or throw light on these acts,—all the acts of others relative to the affair, that come to his knowledge, and may influence him,—his friendships and enmities, his promises, his threats, the truth of his discourses, the falsehood of his apologies, pretences, and explanations, his looks, his speech, his silence where he was called on to speak, everything which tends to establish the connection between all these particulars,—every circumstance, precedent, concomitant, and subsequent, become parts of circumstantial evidence.

The description is finely suited to Trump. His every utterance in response to the inquiry has contained an equivocation—the richest being his assurance to the press on January 15 that "I never *worked for* Russia!" (emphasis added). Consider his dangling a hope of pardon to some friends and his public banishment of others; his forgettings and rememberings, timed for the approach of the next subpoena, and released through Giuliani in different forms on different days; the falsehood, pretense, and contradictory explanations offered concerning the hush money and the Trump Tower Moscow negotiations. The circumstantial evidence is constraining in a precise sense: one can't imagine anyone behaving like this without a purpose. And by now the nature of the plan, if not the particulars, is clear enough. His run for president was meant to widen and intensify his fame in the United States, but he would almost certainly lose the 2016 election. He was counting on that. Meanwhile, he would amass hundreds of millions from a hotel project in Moscow, and leave the bits of treachery scattered and invisible in his wake. Who had the motive or the energy to track an eccentric billionaire already known to be dicey?

The majority of Americans have always been nonpolitical. At an academic conference in Nashville, Tennessee, the weekend before the election, I ducked out one evening with a friend, but the band in the pub was too loud and we took our beers to a fenced-in porch. The talk had slid into predictable anti-Trump musings when a man who stood nearby called out: "Which one of you is the lawyer?" I said I was a teacher not a lawyer, but Robert (as he introduced himself) followed up with another question. "What are you?" "I'm a Democrat." "I'm a Republican," was his answer to start a conversation he'd been wanting to have, "and I voted for Trump. You see those cranes, all the construction going on? We've got work in Nashville and the tax cut helped. I know some of the economy comes from Obama, but I give Trump credit." He added that Trump said what he thought, was fearless, a relief from politicians and so on.

Robert connected his liking for Trump to a work accident. He heads a local union that installs elevators; one of his crew, a friend, had been killed when an elevator fell on him. There was a lot of red tape involved in getting the insurance to pay. At this point, my friend cut in: "Don't you see you're being taken for a ride? The Republicans are the union-busting party. Any progress you're going to make will come from the Democrats." Robert didn't deny it, but his grievance was general: all the inadequacies around insurance companies and, for that matter, unions reminded him of something about Democrats. And here (out of nowhere) came a denunciation of the Clintons. "What was all the money with the Clinton Foundation and Haiti? We'll never know the truth." When I asked where he got his news, the answer was Yahoo. Robert's companion, Billy, who was pretty hammered and had been quiet till now, weighed in with an aphorism: "I vote Republican to preserve my poverty and integrity!" Somehow the name of Trump's Supreme Court nominee, Brett Kavanaugh, came up, and turned the discussion to the mob action around his confirmation hearing. Robert said, "Those people were disgusting." I said, but the right-wing mobs carry weapons and beat people up, that's a whole different category. A young black man from the bar, overhearing us, stepped outside and joined forces with Robert: "The leftist mob, they're bad!"

All in all, it was a peculiar evening, but I suspect the weirdness of it could be matched anywhere in the United States today. Why is it so easy to talk to people like Robert and so hard to change their minds? The Democrats have a language problem. They refer to Trump in clinical jargon as a "narcissistic personality," toss about Greek words like "homophobic" and "misogynistic," "transphobic" and "xeno-phobic," and actually made themselves believe that Trump calling Hillary Clinton "nasty woman" would be a shock-ing story when in most people's minds it was another forgettable piece of bad manners—vulgar, yes, but we knew that. The elevation of abstract language with no salt or savor, and no traction in common speech, the anathemas that come across as finger-wagging, the antiseptic prudery that runs in a pipeline from campuses to center-left journalism and finally to the Democratic Party (where older moderates like Senator Leahy and Senator Durbin seem to have no idea what is happening)—these misjudgments form a pattern with a history. They include such manifestations as Obama's line, "I should have anticipated the optics," to excuse his appearance on the golf course at Martha's Vineyard a few minutes after his statement on the beheading of the war correspondent James Foley. Slips like this are the result of an entrenched complacency that few in the academic-corporate-political-digital elite are ever made aware of. The Me Too saying "Believe all survivors," widely publicized at the Kavanaugh hearing, may be a resonant slogan but it isn't identical with "Treat all accusations seriously." Most Americans still believe that an accused person is innocent until proven guilty; and it would be a moral disaster for Democrats to discard the principle as the condemned property of right-wing libertarians.

The party of Hillary Clinton, National Public Radio, and the *New Yorker* had better mind the increasingly careless deployment of the phrases *white man* and *white male* as dismissive epithets. "They call themselves moderates and problem-solvers, consensus-builders and pragmatists. Monochrome and male, they do not embody social change and few hold out the promise of making history"—so ran a pair of sentences near the start of a *Times* story mocking the absurdly retro views and skin color of Democratic centrists. The reporter is a recent graduate of Harvard whom the *Times* picked up from *Politico*—a symptomatic trajectory. The cliché about making history because you are the first non-white, non-male, non-straight person in some category, exhibits an attitude the Ivies and the 24/7 outlets have projected into mainstream journalism. Again, the annual Women's March in Humboldt County, in northern California, was cancelled in January because the participants were going to be "overwhelmingly white"—a story that got coverage in very different tones of voice depending on the presenter's venue. You don't want the laughter to turn into votes; and the too-white notion has been gaining ground in Democratic circles ever since its use by Hillary Clinton against Bernie Sanders in the 2016 primaries: it was said that as a senator from Vermont, he represented "a very white state." The educational value (if any) of such a reminder is lost on the sensibilities of people (the vast majority of humankind at any moment) who can't be talked into voluntary self-denial on account of their race. The potentially useful suggestion "More black people here would be a good thing" will not be heard where the grammar says, "Too many white people." Giddy with their deserved triumph in 2018, the Democrats and their media allies are pouring fuel on a resentment that could bring another election like 2016.

The cause of the government shutdown in December and January, namely Trump's insistence on money for the wall and the Democratic refusal to supply it, did not vanish with the president's decision to reopen government. Trump looked very bad in this controversy, but the Democratic congressional leaders, Nancy Pelosi and Chuck Schumer, will look almost as bad if they stick to their policy of not-a-dollar-not-an-inch for the wall. They now say the very idea of a wall is "immoral," but stretches of metal fence are built and functioning in San Diego, El Paso, and elsewhere; and Democrats had already signaled their readiness to add more, until Trump upped the ante and made it a mutual test of wills. Why spin out moral maxims in the heat of a merely political contest? By the middle of the shutdown, Trump had surrendered the largest and most picturesque element of his pledge—an unscaleable wall across the entire border, paid for by Mexico—and he has now accepted a compromise appropriation for border security and invoked emergency powers to make up the difference and build his wall. While Democrats challenge this in the courts, Trump will press his side of the standoff from now to November 2020; and good fortune will not attend the party that gets to pick up the pieces. The twin mottos of the woke left, "Abolish ICE" and "No Borders, No Walls," can never win votes in the United States for the same reason they could never win in Britain, France, Germany, China, or Russia. The bland saying "We are a nation of immigrants!" isn't an argument either. What is wanted is a return to humane enforcement and a law by which longtime residents, persons who know no other country as their home, may be provided with a decent path to citizenship.

The shutdown of the government produced bewilderment all around while giving pleasure to the anti-immigration alarmists who provoked it when they called Trump a coward. Democrats leaned heavily on the incivility of the government layoffs and suspension of paychecks, with considerable help from interviews of workers by the mainstream media. This was a fair political signal to liberals, who think well of government workers to begin with, but it couldn't appeal to Republicans and independents who have been taught to despise the needy, to hate government and to inquire no further: the perverse morality of Reaganite common sense. While summoning compassion for the plight of Trump's victims, Democrats might also have pointed out what people were missing in the absence of government. The work stoppage from the shutdown was a chance for the opposition to remind Americans what the government does, and to say to inheritors of the Reaganite contempt: "Now do you begin to see? You *like* the DC museums to be open. You *like* the security lines at the airports to be relatively quick and efficient. You *like* the national parks and the rangers who help you there. You do want your meat inspected and your vegetables checked for poison, and you don't want the post office to be replaced by Trump Delivery Service." People actually need to be told what government is always doing for them.

A fresh direction for the Democratic Party has been left to sources far from its familiar bosses, donors, and ex-presidents. One of the few genuinely dissident figures in Congress, Tulsi Gabbard—an Iraq War veteran and representative for Hawaii—has announced her candidacy in the primaries and made a leading issue her determination to withdraw the US from "regime-change wars." Alexandria Ocasio-Cortez, in collaboration with Senator Ed Markey of Massachusetts, has begun to publicize the environmentalist program for a Green New Deal, which, on the pattern of William James's moral equivalent of war, would divert military resources to retard climate change and build up protection against its effects. The program should have admitted it was all about climate change, instead of

pretending to answer every other problem in the same
stroke, but anyway it is a start. The Senate vote of 68–23
requiring US troops to stay in Afghanistan shows the kind
of strength it will take to complete even the negative part of
such a plan. Trump, in his State of the Union address on
February 5, reassured the country that "there's nothing
anywhere in the world that can compete with America,"
and when he repeated the sentiment—"Members of
Congress, the state of our union is strong"—he was
answered by Republicans in the audience with a chanted
chorus of "USA! USA!" His approval rate in February
climbed to the mid-40s, and even this incoherent speech
got high marks from viewers who liked the mix of unctuous
salutations and lurid Mexican anecdotes, topped off by the
warning that things will go well provided we keep away
from "foolish wars, politics, and ridiculous investigations."
Though he has been an asset, if not an agent, for the Saudis
and Israel and on occasion Russia too, the law he broke
has yet to be named. Reelection seems just as likely as
impeachment. He is fighting for his life, and he would
rather sue than settle.

Conclusion

How do we get it back? Many people asking that question are thinking about more than Donald Trump's offenses against the dignity of high office. They are wondering how, with so much broken already, one man fumbling at the controls could find still more to destroy. In 2016, Trump was cast as the voice of rebellion against a power whose dimensions few understood; and in a campaign that started as a promotional gimmick, he ran a hard race and surprised the country. Russian meddling is unlikely to have swayed the result in a single state, yet the Democrats and their media allies jumped at the idea of the stolen election. The premature fantasy of a quick removal of President Trump—and the comparative slowness with which the real extent of his corruption was brought to light—have enabled the president's backers to play the conspiracy story in reverse: an election Trump legitimately won is about to be retroactively reclaimed by the deep state. The Mueller report when it comes will satisfy neither side. It will lay out illicit connections between Trump and financial and state actors, some American, some Russian, possibly some from other countries. It will hand lawmakers a map from which they can induce a logical path to impeachment, on charges of obstruction and emoluments, and perhaps on other grounds as well; but the report will not overtly recommend impeachment, and its legal upshot will be left to prosecutors in New York and elsewhere who are handling Trump-related indictments. The crowd that continues to support him, united by animosity more than by positive belief, is too formless to become a movement, but it has sufficient size and energy to tear the country apart. So the question returns. Can we recover a rational skepticism regarding the state and corporate institutions that for so long have governed unaccountably, and at the same time acknowledge the value of a representative government with three functioning branches? For constitutional democracy to survive, this doubt and this fidelity must be made to coexist again.

On the Election

November 2016

From the first debates of 2015, Donald Trump stood out because he wasn't one of the usual suspects. He was the to-hell-with-it candidate. If you dislike politics generally, don't study or understand them but are sure the country has declined and that the future looks worse than the past, Trump is your man. He doesn't know politics any better than you do, but he says (reassuringly) that it is a mug's game, and he ought to know. He comes from money, lives for money, and before he entered the race he was in the business of buying favors from the mugs.

Who better to avow that the system is rigged? Everyone admits that the Clinton Foundation has done good works. But anyone with a nose can tell that it uneasily mixes philanthropy and aggrandizement. Trump took his cue and blew it up and—since Hillary Clinton is known to have met with donors while she was secretary of state—he called the foundation itself a pay-to-play scheme. Trump the insider has the best and biggest nose for such things; and in the mood of perpetual disquiet these last two years in America, the undeniable blots on his character have made people strangely trust him more.

Comparisons with Reagan are misleading. Reagan was intimate with politics and political interests as far back as his presidency of the Screen Actors Guild. He tricked his opponents into underrating him, right up to the election of 1980, but the reason wasn't the lack of a consistent ideology or a coherent personality. Reagan was undeviating in his overall views: the people who supported him knew what they were getting. With Trump, they prefer not to know, and he panders to wishful ignorance by saying that whatever he does in his first days as president, he'll do it good and do it fast. The vagueness, bloat, and feckless reiteration of the promises (the height of the wall with Mexico, the total ban on Muslim immigration, the vow to "bring back a hell of a lot worse than waterboarding") go against the grain of a representative government based on checks and self-restraint.

Trump the post-political billionaire can seem refreshingly heterodox only if one performs a drastic curtailment of common judgment. The right-wing anti-imperialist Pat Buchanan thinks that Trump has the mind-set and stamina to extricate the United States from our half-dozen wars in the Greater Middle East (Afghanistan, Iraq, Syria, Yemen, Libya, Somalia). On the evidence, one would guess that Trump indeed has a less hearty appetite for wars than Hillary Clinton, but his solutions often sound like "Bomb them back to the Stone Age" rather than the reasoned noninterventionism this branch of apologists are looking for.

On the other hand, the description of Trump as a pawn of Putin—offered by mainstream and liberal outlets like *Slate*, *Salon*, the *New York Times*, the *New Yorker*, and the *Washington Post*—is a projection of fantasy as palpable as Buchanan's and even more irresponsible. Trump seems to admire Putin as he admires other executives, in business and politics alike, who have proved themselves by building up their success with a flamboyant disregard of rules. We know little more than that.

In the first debate, Clinton was the beneficiary of a total failure of preparation by Trump. Even so, her stated positions and political history leave her unequipped to repel his charges against immigration, the American jobs lost through trade deals, and the scenes of disorder in American cities that followed the killing of black men by police and the killing of police by black men. Hillary Clinton is the reverse of a popular politician—she is more like an ideally dutiful chair of a committee—and it has been an odd feature of the campaign to advertise her as "the most qualified person ever to run for president."

What have qualifications, in this CV-building sense, to do with the traits we look for in a president? If the sane and sensible are bound to vote for Clinton as probably the less dangerous bet, still her errors of judgment as secretary of state remain a disturbing fact. In brutal vulgarity of sentiment, her statement on the mutilation and murder of Muammar Qaddafi, "We came, we saw, he died," and the cackle that followed the proclamation are barely matched by Trump's saying of his failure to pay taxes: "That makes me smart."

The disaster of Clinton's policy of regime change in Libya and her desire to repeat the experiment in Syria are the most vulnerable points in her candidacy. But they won't be a major issue in November, because Republicans have cared only about a fraction of the catastrophe, the deaths of four Americans in Benghazi. A larger and more elusive weakness is that she exudes entitlement, of a meritocratic sort, and seems to lack a shred of feeling for people who played by the rules and haven't been crowned with success.

The exceptions are the needy and minorities; but that only reinforces the sense that Democrats treat with contempt those whom they cannot patronize. How many non-elite white voters can now be drawn by Trump to vote with their resentment of the selective compassion of liberals? Trump, of all people, with his trademark saying "You're fired," has turned into the candidate of people who feel they have lost out but don't know why—the people Nathanael West called "the cheated."

The domestic state of the nation is so unpropitious in October 2016 that one may pity the winner of this election as much as the loser. We are living in a country under recurrent siege by the actions of crowds. There is the Tea Party crowd with their belief that global climate disruption is a scientific hoax; there is the Black Lives Matter crowd with their ambiguous slogan "No Justice, No Peace"; and there are more ominous developments, such as the acts of serial defiance of the federal government by the Bundy family in Nevada and Oregon. Whoever comes next will have the task of restoring respect for the law and a common adherence to the Constitution—the heaviest of burdens, even for a candidate prepared by training and disposition to carry it.

APPENDIX B

Bomb First

April 2017

For an American president, bombing is easier than thinking. For an American lawmaker or opinion maker, it costs
nothing to celebrate the resolve of a president who bombs.
On the evening of April 6, Donald Trump reversed his
apparent policy of declining to attack the Assad regime
and fired fifty-nine Tomahawk missiles at a Syrian government airfield. The cause was a report that the Syrian air
force had dropped a chemical bomb that killed at least
seventy-two civilians. John McCain and Lindsey
Graham—who have been among Trump's most strident
critics in the Republican Party, and who have long been
calling for the overthrow of Bashar al-Assad—immediately
applauded the action. The House minority leader, Nancy
Pelosi, approved it as "proportional." Trump's rapid and
definitive response was likewise praised by Fareed Zakaria:
"I think Donald Trump became president" by bombing—a

true president at last (he meant) after weeks of dithering and confusion. Ezra Klein also gave a qualified justification of the missile strike against a nation that has never attacked the United States: Trump had acted "well within the norms of American foreign policy."

This was a peculiar turn of fortune. A president who for many months, both before he won the election and after, had been characterized as dangerously unstable by the people he calls the establishment, now witnessed the same establishment promote him to the ranks of the sane and responsible. What conclusion will be drawn by the mind of Donald Trump?

There was a risk in the sudden violence. Syria is a battle-field in which Russia, too, has fought and built up military assets and invested considerable diplomatic prestige. But Trump had taken the precaution of warning the Russians to clear their people from the target area; and when a Russian UN envoy was asked what he meant when he warned of "negative consequences" of the bombing, he chose not to mention US-Russian relations. He said: "Look at Iraq, look at Libya."

By the end of George W. Bush's second term, the Iraq war had displaced almost five million people in a country of 27 million. By the end of Obama's second term, the Libya war had displaced 400,000 in a country of six million. These are facts the world may choose not to forget as quickly as Americans often do. Five or six years ago, it was the satirical usage of a few critics to speak of "multiple wars" or "perpetual war"; but mainstream journalists now speak casually of how an adviser or a general needs credibility for "our next war." But look at Iraq, look at Libya.

Coverage of the chemical attack in Syria—and of the American missile strike that issued as a "punishment" of Assad to enforce "international norms"—was apparently supported by evidence satisfying to journalists and editors. But here, as in the treatment of secret information about Trump and Russia, there was an order of logic in the reporting that should have set off an alarm. For something new was happening in both cases: the major newspapers, networks, and websites vouched for *conclusions*—regarding the accuracy of the inferences about Trump; regarding the source and motive of the chemical attack in Syria—which they described as having been drawn from a sound interpretation of solid evidence. Yet only conclusions were disclosed. The evidence was revealed in the broadest outlines and with little effort to trace the path by which it acquired legitimacy. So, in the latest instance in Syria, the most clear-cut evidence provided to reporters was simply "an image of the radar track of a Syrian airplane leaving the airfield and flying to the chemical strike area Tuesday." It was assumed by reporters that this meant the use of chemical weapons had been ordered by Assad and that the incident followed a regular pattern of chemical attacks by the Syrian government. The last assumption, however, was exceedingly careless.

The documented attacks that the reporters seemed to have in mind occurred on March 19, 2013, near Aleppo, when more than two dozen were killed; on August 21, 2013, in Ghouta, near Damascus, when many hundreds died of chemical poisoning; and (exactly two years later) on August 21, 2015, in the town of Marea, north of Aleppo. A Reuters story by Anthony Deutsch on November 6, 2015 summarized the conclusion by the Organisation for the Prohibition of Chemical Weapons that banned weapons had indeed been used; the same story revealed the uncertainty of the investigating body concerning which side had used the weapons. Deutsch spoke of "a growing body of evidence that the Islamic State group has obtained, and is using, chemical weapons in both Iraq and Syria." These indications have scarcely been mentioned in recent US reporting on Syria. The Canadian prime minister Justin Trudeau may have had them in mind when, in his initial response to the recent incident, he said that there are "continuing questions . . . about who is responsible for these horrible attacks."

None of this affects what Americans should think of Bashar al-Assad. Before the war began, Assad was one more regional despot like Saddam Hussein and Muammar Qaddafi; though oppressive and illiberal, he posed no international threat. In the civil war, Assad and his allies, Hezbollah, Iran, and Russia, have committed atrocities and inflicted suffering on the Syrian population on a scale that can never be atoned for. His enemies—ISIS, al-Nusra (the Syrian branch of al-Qaeda), and various proxy warriors bankrolled by Turkey, Qatar, and Saudi Arabia—have often done the same. Which of these parties you hate the most, if you are Syrian, may depend on which has killed the largest numbers of your family.

Now, more than five years into this intractable conflict, is it plausible that the United States can alleviate the sufferings caused by Assad—and by his enemies, too—with a full-scale military attempt to overthrow the government of Syria? The American establishment seems to have answered almost overnight with an automatic yes. But the execution of this policy, while keeping us in the fight against ISIS, would add to our list of enemies the other most formidable military powers in the country, namely the armed forces of Syria, Iran's proxies, and Russia. The stated object of the policy would be to stop the bloodshed, but it would entail a drastic acceleration of violence.

Go back a moment to the lesson that Trump is apt to learn from events of the past week. Would it be wrong to reduce it to the following? "You can make some highly respectable new friends by throwing missiles at an obnoxious foreign power. It works like a dream so long as you do it fast and give it a humanitarian gloss." In the sheer quantity of the attention paid, and the narrowness of the attention, something terrible about our political culture has come to light. Consider the *New York Times* on April 7. The morning edition featured no fewer than nineteen stories on the Syria missile strike, with headlines varied and supple: "Anguish Sways the Isolationist"; "A 'Significant Blow' to U.S. Ties, Putin Says"; "A One-Time Strike Aimed at Halting Use of Nerve Gas"; "63 Hours: From Sarin Attack to Missiles Falling"; "Trump Fires a Warning Shot in the Bannon-Kushner Battle"; "An Unexpected Change of Subject at an Elegant Diplomatic Dinner"; "Trump's View of Syria: How It Evolved, in Tweets"; "Trump's Decision Has Some Critics Cheering and Some Supporters Booing"; "GOP Lawmakers, Once Skeptical of Obama Plan to Strike Syria, Back Trump"; "Was Missile Attack on Syria Illegal? Explaining Presidential War Powers"; "Syrians Opposed to Assad Feel Sense of Satisfaction, but Also Fear Reprisals"; "Once Critical of President, Refugees Offer Approval"; "A

Global Divide Over a Missile Attack"; "Missile Strike Signals a New Reality in Syria for Friends and Foes Alike"; "Measuring Action Against a Government Already Under Siege"; "Wasn't Syria's Stock of Chemical Weapons Destroyed? It's Complicated"; "Asking If U.S. Remarks Helped Embolden Assad"; "Who Was in the Room with Him? Trump's Advisers During the Strike"; "For Tillerson and McMaster, Action on Syria Is Chance to Step Out of the Shadows."

The headlines are a shade less redundant than the stories themselves; but the words that inevitably stand out are *attack, strike, decision, action, Syria, Syrians,* and (most of all) *Trump.* Though a critical note is struck in some places, along with a show of scruple concerning the balance between executive action and constitutional law (with law on the whole portrayed sympathetically), the overall message is never in doubt. The newspaper of record is telling a president whose legitimacy it has challenged ever since the election—a president who craves approval almost as much as he loves attention—"Now you have made yourself important in a good way."

Democratic lawmakers have done much the same: Senator Chuck Schumer, when he gave the questionably legal Tomahawk attack his vote of confidence last Thursday, was only following the path of Richard Gephardt when in October 2002 he stood beside George W. Bush in the Rose Garden to display a unified front supporting a possible war against Iraq. Indeed, in the years since 2002, there has not been a Middle East war for which the United States did not invoke a humanitarian motive: to free Afghanistan from the religious tyranny of the Taliban; to create a multicultural democracy in Iraq, in which Kurds, Shiites, and Sunnis could participate equally; to allow the Arab Spring to flourish in Libya by awarding the rebels the victory they deserved. From the Libya catastrophe, Barack Obama may have learned something but his party learned nothing.

Meanwhile, it looks as if the relentless Democratic strategy of pinning Trump to Russia has turned back to plague its inventors. Denigration of Putin and all things Russian was the necessary means to delegitimate Trump, as the Democrats saw it, but the end in view was the destruction of Trump. Weirdly, the Democrats lost sight of this and now Trump has gone up against Putin and rallied the Democrats to back him. They are left holding Trump as their indispensable ally and humanitarian war as a favorite cause, which at an opportune moment could displace any other: the cause of planetary destruction through climate change, for example.

Put this down to a lack of political talent and consistent thinking. The larger discouraging fact is that almost by definition, a member of today's Democratic Party has no interest in foreign policy. However clouded by militarism the judgment of senators like McCain and Graham and their understudy Tom Cotton may be—and however simple and sweeping the nonintervention doctrine of Rand Paul— these Republicans actually have information and opinions they are ready to espouse. Democrats have more to say about Obamacare and abortion and trans bathrooms than they do about Iraq, Syria, Yemen, or Russia. But what you can do at home is limited by the energy and dollars given to enterprises abroad. In February, the Defense Department reported that over the past two and a half years, the United

States has spent $11.9 billion fighting ISIS alone: an average of $12.8 million per day.

On April 9, on the CNN news show *GPS*, General David Petraeus summoned Americans to a lengthened Syrian war. It would not, he said, be a war lasting just a few years beyond 2017, but "a generational struggle," a venture that would require us to measure out in careful quantities the necessary "blood and treasure." Petraeus may yet run for president. He is looking ahead to a merger between a new cold war and a great-power scramble for the Middle East. In response to this extraordinary proposal, his interviewer, Fareed Zakaria, offered no challenge and no question.

The Making of Donald Trump

May 2017

The Making of Donald Trump, a biography and fire alarm, provides a short tour of the business career of America's forty-fifth president. The narrative is episodic and inconsecutive, but it begins at the beginning, with the example set by Fred Trump, the father of Donald: a mid-century real-estate buccaneer, adroit at political manipulation and statute dodging. The book goes on to recount a few of the scandalous details of the construction of Trump Tower and the purchase, mismanagement, and financial collapse of Donald's casino properties in Atlantic City.

Various chapters take in the mob connections that Trump aimed to profit from while keeping at two removes (sometimes with the help of an apartment gratis); there are also free-standing anecdotes about friends and associates, and a chapter on Trump's bid for the gambling custom of the high-rolling Japanese real-estate investor Akio

Kashiwagi. The book bears the marks of having been put together under pressure to stop the election disaster. Pared down to half its length and distributed to every voter in the contested states, it might have helped to produce a different result.

David Cay Johnston, who recently made headlines by releasing a portion of Trump's 2005 tax return, knows whatever can be known about Trump's career, which he covered as a journalist for three decades, and he has the necessary courage for the disagreeable work. Trump's previous biographer—the *Village Voice* city reporter Wayne Barrett, who died in January—gave a definitive account of the president's first two grown-up decades in *Trump: The Deals and the Downfall* (1992). Both biographers acquired an intimate knowledge of Trump's self-protective method, which involves a mixture of flattery, threat, and bluster. Trump once called Johnston and told him if he didn't like what he wrote, he would sue him; when Johnston reminded Trump that he was a public figure, Trump said: "I'll sue you anyway."

With Barrett, whose book was long in the making and four times the size of Johnston's, the stakes were higher and the approach subtler. Trump said that he couldn't help knowing his biographer lived in a modest apartment in a nothing neighborhood; and by the way, he, Trump, had some very nice apartments on offer. When this failed to draw a response, Trump told the sad story of another journalist who had written copy he disliked. I took him to court and broke him, said Trump.

Johnston moved to Atlantic City in 1988 to report for the *Philadelphia Inquirer* on the spread of casinos, after a

Supreme Court ruling that Indian tribes had a right to own them. He was convinced the mob would pursue the new market, and "I quickly learned from others in town that [Trump] knew next to nothing about the casino industry, including the rules of the games." On this subject and others, Johnston played the trick of intentionally saying something false in order to get Trump to agree and betray his ignorance.

"Net present value" is a precise business term that means "the value of cash expected from an investment minus the value spent to support that investment and then reduced to a lump sum payable today." Under cross-examination in court, Trump (who sued the reporter Tim O'Brien for saying his net present value might be far below the $5–$6 billion he claimed) strayed early and began to blow smoke: "Well, to me, the word 'net' is an interesting word. It's really—the word 'value' is the important word." Trump has been "a party in more than 3,500 lawsuits," remarks Johnston—an act of hostile sociability as typical of the man as the tweets he emits at four a.m. The lawsuit against O'Brien, like all the others presumably, was worth it because of the trouble it cost his enemy: "I spent a couple of bucks on legal fees and they spent a whole lot more. I did it to make his life miserable, which I'm happy about."

When Trump became interested in Atlantic City, he summoned the New Jersey attorney general and asked for early action, which would mean shortcuts on the background checks. Clear this for me (Trump said in effect) or I won't build in Atlantic City; and by the way, I own space in New York that would be just as good for a casino. The Division of Gaming Enforcement bought his pitch without, it is said, ever notifying the Casino Control Commission that Trump had been the target of federal criminal investigations. Once a Trump success or the appearance of success is given plausibility by banks, and by city or state governments, he has his hooks in the institutions and they can't afford to let him sink. When his Atlantic City casinos went bankrupt, he was judged too big to fail by the state of New Jersey. The punishment was to put him on a monthly allowance of $450,000.

If a single story emerges, it is the complicity of financial institutions in every stage of the rise and the resurrection of Trump. For a reader who before 2016 knew him only as a sketchy figure in the world of real estate, fake wrestling, and reality TV, the extent of the connivance is shocking. In *Trump: The Art of the Deal*, the book he wrote in 1987 with Tony Schwartz, Trump claimed to have paid $5 million in cash for the purchase of Mar-a-Lago, but in court testimony, Johnston says, he later "confirmed that his primary bank, Chase Manhattan, had loaned him the entire purchase price." The transaction had the peculiar legal status of "a non-recorded mortgage." But surely a mortgage needs a guarantor? Trump said he "personally guaranteed" the loan to himself by Chase Manhattan. The next page tightens the analogy between his practices and those that triggered the 2008 financial collapse: "Many banks," Johnston writes, "complained that they were unaware other banks had loaned money to Trump on his personal guarantee with no public record of the obligation." Years before he ran for president, Trump was a human complex derivative.

His lesser stratagems have required neither treachery nor the concealment of relevant facts. They exhibit nothing worse than a shameless use of the legal resources for squeezing extra dollars through the tax loopholes available to the very rich (especially the landed rich). Trump could reduce the property tax on his golf course in Bedminster, New Jersey, almost down to zero by keeping a pen of goats there and having it zoned as "active farmland."

More inventively, he gave orders to skip tenth-floor numbers "to inflate the apparent height of his signature building." Much of the remaining 90 percent of the apparent height of Trump Tower was built by illegal Polish construction workers who were underpaid. This would involve him later in an unpleasant rigmarole of legal discovery and compensation, but when he had money on his mind, his associates have observed, "common sense just never took hold." In the 2016 campaign, he paid himself for the use of his large and small private jets, his helicopter, and his office space in Trump Tower.

The biggest mistake of the Clinton strategy that lost the 2016 election was to picture Trump as a misogynist, racist, and general offender against the international regime of human rights. While Trump can be relied on to pick up any prejudice opportunistically and pat and stroke it as long as it serves his interest, his racism and a deeper strain of misogyny hardly stand out in the Republican Party today. No: the egregious fact is his business record. Yet somehow the Democrats reckoned that the business facts about Trump were already known. Hillary Clinton mentioned now and then that he had stiffed people he hired to work for him. The campaign should have driven that point home in every speech she made and every ad they ran. Trump's conduct in the first four months of his presidency bears out the suspicion that he will treat the legal institutions of the United States the way he treated the New Jersey Division of Gaming Enforcement.

"Mr. Trump," the lawyer asked in the net worth trial, "have you always been completely truthful in your public statements about your net worth of properties?" This curious exchange ensued: "I try," Trump answered. "Have you ever not been truthful?" "My net worth fluctuates, and it goes up and down with markets and with attitudes and with feelings, even my own feelings, but I try." A few months into his presidency, many people have stopped wondering about Trump's fluctuations of policy, and have begun to ask a more unsettling question: who controls his feelings?

Acknowledgments

Thanks are due to the editors of the *London Review of Books*, the *New York Review of Books, Harper's,* and the *Guardian* for articles that first appeared in those journals. Since the chapters add up to a sort of political diary, I have made only minor corrections and cut some but not all repetitions. Note should be made of the time-lag between the writing and the listed dates of publication. The chapter on the Obama presidency, "What Went Wrong," for example, came out in June 2015 but was drafted in March and April; "On the Election," written in late October 2016, was published in an issue dated after the election; the conclusion comes from the interval between President Trump's declaration of emergency powers and the submission of the Mueller report. I am sometimes asked where to find useful information that is ignored or abridged in the conventional outlets. Among the most valuable resources, for me, have been *Antiwar, Counterpunch, Democracy Now!,* Digby's *Hullabaloo, Empty Wheel,* the *Intercept, LobeLog, Mondoweiss,* and *Tom Dispatch.* For help on the way, I owe much to Gilman Anderson, Christopher Beha, Mark and Paul Bromwich, Karen and Ned Duval, Hugh Eakin, Deborah Friedell, Seymour Hersh, George Kateb, Paul Laity, Christopher Lydon, the late Robert Silvers, Mary-Kay Wilmers, and Georgann Witte. Jake Stevens at Verso had the idea for this book, and I am very grateful for his encouragement. Emily Albarillo assisted with exact and timely copy-editing, and Mark Martin has my warm appreciation for seeing the manuscript through to press.

Index